CW00797176

IF I WERE YOUR WIFE

LOTTA LUNDGREN

NEW HOLLAND

Published in 2012 by New Holland Publishers Ltd
London • Cape Town • Sydney • Auckland
www.newhollandpublishers.com

Garfield House, 86-88 Edgware Road, London W2 2EA, London
Wembley Square First Floor Solan Road Gardens Cape Town 8001 South Africa
Unit 1, 66 Gibbes Street, Chatswood, NSW 2067, Australia
218 Lake Road, Northcote, Auckland, New Zealand

First published in Sweden in 2011 by Norstedts
as OM JAG VAR DIN HEMMAFRU © Lotta Lundgren 2011
English translation © 2012 New Holland Publishers (UK) Ltd

A catalogue record for this book is available from the British Library.

ISBN 978 178009 152 5

Text and recipes © *Lotta Lundgren*
Graphic design: *Karin Ahlgren* and *Lotta Mårlind*
Final art: *Beatrice Sztanska*
Photographs © *Pelle Bergström*
Photographer's assistant: *Magnus Torsne*
Image processing: *Jenny Widingsjö*. Portrait retouch: *Johan Cabbe Cabezos*
Portrait styling: *Sofia Ronthén*. Hair and makeup: *Sara Denman*
Production director: *Olga Dementiev*
Printing by: *Toppan Leefung (China) Ltd*

10 9 8 7 6 5 4 3 2 1

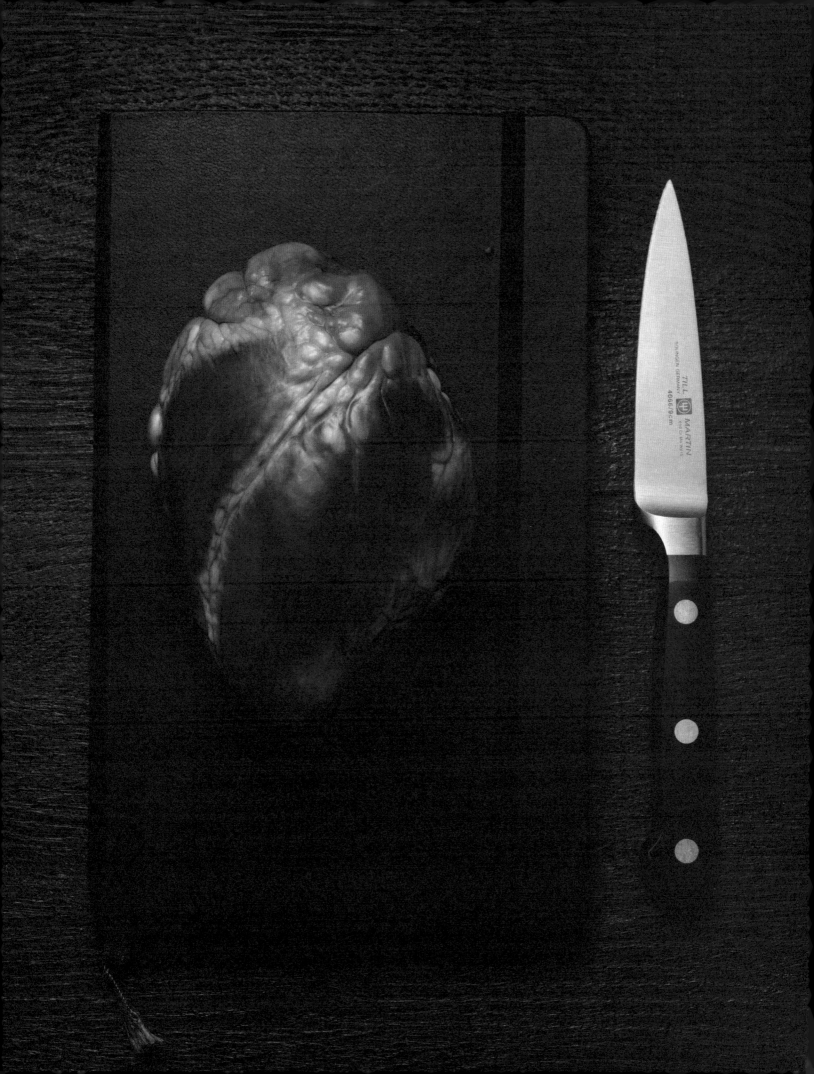

Contents

" The highlight of my childhood was
 making my brother laugh so hard that
 food came out of his nose."

Garrison Keillor

Basic recipes *and some friendly housewifely advice*

Bechamel

Bechamel is a basic white sauce used in a number of dishes such as lasagne and moussaka or for fillings when making crepes. If you add Parmesan cheese, it turns into a cheese sauce. If you exchange the milk for cream and add white wine, white pepper and French tarragon you have a white wine sauce that is delicious with fish.

¾oz (25g) butter, 2 tablespoons plain flour, 1 cup (8¾fl oz/250ml) milk, pinch of salt

In a pot, melt the butter. Turn down heat and add flour while whisking. Add milk 2¾fl oz (100ml) at a time and let thicken while stirring. Add salt. Let bubble for a few minutes while stirring (it takes away the floury taste).

Home made flatbreads

Do what? Fry *dough* right on the stove in a frying pan? Why would anyone do that, you may wonder. To which I reply: Because it's cosy and comforting and this bread goes so well with the majority of the soups and stews in this book.

24oz (750g) plain flour, 1 teaspoon salt, 2 teaspoons sugar, ½ teaspoon baking soda, 2 teaspoons yeast powder, 7fl oz (200ml) milk, 2¾fl oz (100ml) yogurt, 1 egg, 2 tablespoons oil

Mix all dry ingredients in a bowl. Heat the milk until it's lukewarm. Add milk, yogurt, egg and oil to flour mixture and mix into a dough. Let rise under cover for an hour. Shape into large, flat rounds and pile on top of each other between slightly greased baking sheets. Leave to rise for 20 more minutes.
   Are you the happy owner of a pizza stone? Great? Place it on a grid in the upper part of the oven and crank up the heat to maximum grill. Bake off one bread at a time with baking sheet and all, right on the stone, for about 3 minutes or until they puff up and take on a nice colour. If you're not the owner of a pizza stone (most of us fall into this category), heat some oil in a frying pan and fry the breads until they puff up and take on a nice colour on both sides. If you like, you can keep the fried breads warm in the oven at 250°F (120°C/Gas Mark 1), but not for long—you don't want these breads too dry.

On cooking beans

You may have been told that dried beans must be put aside to soak overnight then cooked for what seems like an eternity, a procedure so laborious you'd rather buy them ready cooked. But if you add a little baking soda to the soaking water, you could cut the cooking time in half. If you don't have time to soak your beans, try my express method that yields ready cooked beans with skins intact and a tender interior!
   Empty the entire package of dried beans into a large pot. Add water—as much as your pot can take without boiling over. *WHATEVER YOU DO, DO NOT ADD SALT!* Bring to a boil under lid and let simmer for 30 minutes (never mind if the kitchen gets all steamy, humid air is great for your skin). Turn the hob off but let the pot remain in place until the water has cooled off. Now taste! If the beans are still a little too hard, bring them to yet another boil, turn the hob off and let stand to cool. Gently rinse the beans, use immediately or freeze in plastic bags or well-cleaned milk cartons.

On cooking pasta

Perfectly cooked pasta has a little bit of resistance left when you chew it and doesn't turn into a sticky ball in the bottom of your pot as soon as you bring it to the table. The next time you cook pasta, ladle up a cupful of the boiling water when the pasta is almost done and add a generous knob of butter to it. Drain the pasta in a colander then bring it back into the pot. Add the buttered water, stir and serve, triumphantly.

Garlic puree

Is it all right to steal from the nobility? Can you cook without garlic? Is there something immoral about rationalising away one of the most finicky, tedious and repetitive of chores? These matters have been discussed for centuries. Whatever your stand is, I would like you to know that oven roasted garlic gets all creamy, sweet and mild with a great slightly burnt taste, and that it is very handy to drop down into whatever you're cooking compared to having to peel, chop and fry garlic cloves.

5 garlic bulbs, 2¾fl oz (100ml) olive oil, pinch of salt

Break up the garlic bulbs and sit the cloves (yes, peels and all) evenly on a baking sheet. Roast in oven at 350°F (180°C/Gas Mark 4), for 20 minutes. Remove the peels, put cloves in a food processor or mixer together with olive oil and salt and mix until smooth. One teaspoon of puree equals about one clove of garlic. If you keep the puree in a clean glass jar in a cold place, it will last for weeks.

Stock

I used to think making your own stock was an activity only someone with too much time and a poor self-image would even think of. Then one day, I made some stock myself and realised home cooked stock is the closest we'll get to a magic brew. You make stock from things you would otherwise have thrown away. And in return for the minimal effort you put in to making it, you're rewarded with a taste enhancer ready to be added to any sauce, stew or soup that could use a boost.

Vegetable stock

Clean out your veggie drawer: even ones that look a little tired and sad now get the chance to shine! You can use almost any vegetable or root that has some taste (with the exception of cabbage and those wrinkly potatoes). If you're fond of cooking Asian style, feel free to flavour stock with ginger, chilli, citrus, lemongrass or lime leaves.

SUITABLE INGREDIENTS:
Leftover stalks from FRESH HERBS. CARROTS, peeled and sliced. PARSNIP, peeled and sliced. ONIONS, coarsely chopped with skin, LEEKS, remove base of the root, slice the rest. GARLIC, chop coarsely with skin and all. GINGER, do not peel—slice finely. ORGANIC LEMON, the juice or entire fruit cut in chunks. ORGANIC ORANGE, see lemon. FRESH CHILLI, slice finely and be careful—don't use too much. LEMONGRASS, well pounded. LIME LEAVES, shred to get the most out of the flavour.

RHUBARB thickens stock and gives a somewhat tart flavour that makes it a fantastic choice for stews containing pork. CELERY STALKS, be careful with the amount you add to make sure the celery taste doesn't overpower everything else. CELERIAC, peeled and diced, also, the warning issued for celery stalk above applies here too. TOMATOES, add nice colour and acidity. BELL PEPPER, coarsely chopped, core and all. BEETROOT, add a little piece of this if you find pink stock appealing.

Cut the vegetables in coarse chunks, pack tightly in a big glass jar with lid, fill up with water all the way to the top, and place the jar in an equally tall pot. Fill the cooking pot with water and let everything simmer on low heat for about 30 minutes. Put aside to cool. Once cool, lift out the jar and strain to remove the vegetable. Keep the stock in a glass jar with lid or freeze as ice cubes.

Meat stock

Bones or chicken carcass or suitable leftovers from your dinner, let it get a second chance in your home-cooked meat stock. If there's sufficient space in your freezer it's a great idea to make a large batch. Fry carcass and bones in a frying pan, or roast in 500°F (250°C/Gas Mark 9) oven at grill setting for about 20 minutes. Transfer to a large stockpot, pour over water, add a peeled chopped onion and, if you like, a few bay leaves and some pepper corns. Cover and let simmer for an hour, then remove lid and let simmer until reduced to half the original amount. Let cool and once cold, remove and discard the fat that collects at the surface. Keep the stock in a glass jar with lid or freeze as ice cubes.

Shellfish stock

Roast shrimp shells in a roasting pan in the oven at 500°F (250°C/Gas Mark 9), grill setting, for about 10 minutes, or until you simply can't take the stench any longer. Transfer to a pot, add one chopped onion, add enough water to cover and let simmer for an hour. Strain to remove the shells. If the stock looks cloudy, bring to a boil, add one egg white and whisk like a maniac. Strain again. Use immediately or keep in your refrigerator.

Sauerkraut

If hope is the last thing that dies in a man (or woman), what is the next to last thing to die? If you ask me, my reply is: a sense of humour. Once you're done smoking that philosophical cigar, let us shift our focus and interest to the first thing that dies in a man (or woman). What is that? Is it civility? Sententiousness? Or simply the ambition to *eat more sauerkraut*?

I admit that sauerkraut doesn't really have its name going for it, but it is all the same a wonderful addition to almost all hearty meals. Making your own sauerkraut doesn't require much. You really only need:

A) a strong and true desire to eat sauerkraut
B) cabbage
C) a large pot for the cabbage

D) non-iodised salt, and

E) a large stone. The stone is of vital importance. If you don't have a large stone, you'll end up with no sauerkraut. You see, you need something heavy to press down on the cabbage so that the sourness is released in a convincing way. You'll find stones in Scotland or Ireland. There are a more urban kind too, often used at outdoor parking lots. I think it's OK to steal stones if it serves a higher purpose.

This is how you make sauerkraut. Halve and slice the entire head of your cabbage as finely as you can—the finer, the better. Put the cabbage on a flat surface and pound it with a rolling pin. Sprinkle salt over the pounded cabbage and taste to make sure that it is about as salty as sauerkraut usually is. Pack the cabbage tightly in the bottom of a large pot, cover with a plate and place the stone on top. Drape a tea towel over the whole pot and let it stand for a week in room temperature or somewhat colder. Once the cabbage has juiced and acquired a delightful sour quality it is time to transfer it to clean glass jars. Keep in refrigerator.

Staples
From my experience, it is advisable to always keep a basic assortment of spices, perishables, rice, pasta and tinned foods at home so that you don't have to run down to the grocery store every time you want to cook. Exactly what you should keep in your cupboard is naturally depending on what kind of cooking you fancy. If you appreciate the kind of food represented in this book, your list of essentials could look something like this:

1. Lemon, organic. 2. Garlic. 3. Onion. 4. Ginger, fresh. 5. Walnuts. Keep them in the freezer—applies to all nuts. 6. Almonds. 7. Cashew nuts. 8. Pine nuts. 9. Feta cheese, authentic Greek. 10. Parmesan, Parmigiano Reggiano. 11. Butter. 12. Olive oil or canola oil. 13. Balsamic vinegar (high-quality). 14. Sesame oil. 15. Asian fish sauce. 16. Japanese soy sauce. 17. Chinese soy sauce. 18. Wine, red and white. 19. Black pepper, whole, to be ground in pepper mill. 20. Regular salt. 21. Flake salt. 22. Cinnamon, whole sticks. 23. Cinnamon, ground. 24. Star anise. 25. Cardamom, whole seeds. 26. Cumin, ground. 27. Chilli, fresh. Keep in freezer, so you always have it at home. 28. Chilli, dried 29. Stock cubes (buy a non-MSG variety). 30. Panko, see Asian grocery stores. 31. All kinds of canned tomatoes, preferably organic. 32. Coconut milk. 33. Beans and lentils, dried and ready cooked. 34. Pasta. 35. Basmati rice. 36. Wholegrain rice. 37. Couscous and/or bulgur. 38. Plain flour.

Asian grocery stores
The problem with Asian food stores is that many people become so overwhelmed with the generous supply of foreign treats that they rarely manage to walk out with much more than the requisite bag of shrimp crisps. I'm not saying everything in an Asian grocery store is for everyone, but a few things are too great and versatile to miss.

Learn this list by heart and ask the staff if you need help in finding things:

1. Asian fish sauce. Ask for the yummiest kind. 2. Panko. Japan's answer to breadcrumbs. 3. Lime leaves. You'll find these in the freezer. 4. Sesame oil. Buy the best you can find, even if it's expensive. 5. Dried chilli. Hot, cheap and great. 6. Dried shiitake and Chinese mushrooms. If you like mushrooms. 7. Soba noodles. Expensive, delicious, Japanese buckwheat noodles.

Beauty treatments

At the end of a stressful day, pamper yourself with a cooling, firming facemask in the shape of a comfortingly cool, half-emptied bag-in-box, liberated from its box and then draped over the face. Let it work its magic on your face for at least 10 minutes.

Zen Buddhism

If you're not a housewife yourself—or if you don't have one, if you're just a regular person with a job and children to attend to—everyday life is rarely the context best suited for new and adventurous cooking. Trust me, it's a far better idea to stick to a limited number of everyday favourites, food you can cook in your sleep, according to a nice and tidy schedule.

Select 10 dishes you know and like. Write down the order on a piece of paper and put it on your fridge. Make sure you have all the basic ingredients at home. Then rejoice in the harmony and inner peace that comes with cooking when it's a meditative moment instead of a stressful chore.

If you can't come up with a single great everyday recipe, feel free to try mine. You'll find suitable dishes on pages 22, 23, 28, 29, 31, 38, 41, 44, 45, 48, 51, 54, 58, 65, 87, 88, 105, 112, 118, 120, 143, 158, 161 and 165.

Refrigerator roulette

Many common misconceptions are fuelled by cookbooks (see above), such as the idea that people should cook and eat real dishes every day of the week.

There is no truth to this at all. A meal is simply this: someone sits down to eat something. This something can be a mix of all sorts of things you find in your fridge or cupboard. Fry something, cook something, boil something, add some cheese and nuts and put it on the table. If it's Friday (or you'd like to create a Friday feeling any other day of the week), you can arrange your various treats into pretty little bowls and serve as festive tapas.

All recipes in this book are intended to serve *4 PEOPLE*, unless otherwise stated. I use large organic eggs, regular, salted butter, nothing but organic lemons and oranges and aged Parmesan cheese.

You can use canola oil instead of olive oil if you want to, but no matter which one you decide on I strongly recommend that you pick a variety of a higher quality than the cheapest kind around.

A *can* of this or a *package* of that means a can or a package of the most common kind. And when I write a *chilli* of either colour, I refer to the fresh, long and narrow, medium heat kind you'll find in the nearest store. The amount of butter or oil used for frying, salt and freshly ground pepper is rarely mentioned in the recipe ingredient list. If you wonder why, please read further on page 81. *Now, food!*

Believe me, this ratatouille is so easy to make *it is absurd*. I can assure you that you'll whip it up in fifteen minutes as you tidy up the apartment (with a kid on your hip), unload the dishwasher, read the editorials, reschedule lunch for next Tuesday, polish your silverware, compose a few arty still lifes AND do your Kegels. The only obstacle to this fine arrangement would be if you insisted on making the sausage yourself from animals that you personally hunt down in the forest.

Ratatouille *with goat's cheese and chorizo*

Preheat the oven to 440°F (225°C/Gas Mark 7) grill.

Halve the tomatoes, mince the garlic, slice the onion, peel, trim and dice the remaining vegetables.

Sweat the garlic and onion in olive oil in a pot for a few minutes, add aubergine (eggplant) and pepper (capsicum) and let fry until they begin to soften. While they putter on, rinse the lemons and zest them both (be light on your hand—only the outermost yellow part of the peel) but only juice one. Add zest, lemon juice, sugar, tomatoes and thyme leaves. Season with salt, pepper, lemon juice and freshly ground pepper.

Cut the goat's cheese in two hefty slices, then halve those too so that you end up with

13oz (400g) cherry
  tomatoes
4 garlic cloves
1 red onion
1 small aubergine
  (eggplant)
3 bell peppers
  (capsicum), not green
2 lemons
1 tablespoon sugar
  or honey
½–1 pot fresh thyme
7oz (200g) goat's
  cheese
3½oz (100g) olives
  with pits
4 chorizos

4 goat's cheese crescents. Transfer the ratatouille to an ovenproof dish, add the olives and place the cheese on top of it all.

Let the dish cook through in oven for about 10 minutes or until the goat's cheese has changed from plain white to a beautiful, slightly golden colour.

Fry the sausages and serve with the ratatouille.

Let's make a scale. On the one end, we place *My body is my temple*. At the opposite end of the scale, we put *My body is my basement recreation room which I use to store garbage*. Now let's focus on the very centre of the scale. Did you find it? Great. Now follow the dotted vertical line all the way down to the small, nitpicky piece of text below, the text that reads as follows: *My body is my retirement home*. The moral of this story? Eat more vegetables.

Baked bell peppers (capsicum) *with toasted couscous*

Preheat the oven to 440°F (225°C/Gas Mark 7) grill.

Cut a lid off each pepper (capsicum) and remove the seeds and core. Chop the onion finely and the garlic even finer before cooking them in butter for a few minutes over medium heat. Add the uncooked couscous and fry while stirring until the grains start to turn golden. Crumble the stock cube between your fingers into the pot, remove from the heat, pour over the water, put the lid back and leave the couscous to swell.

If you're using frozen corn, rinse it to let it thaw a little before mixing it into the couscous. Grate and add the cheese, but set about one-quarter of the cheese aside for later.

Taste and season with salt, freshly ground black pepper and chipotle (no chipotle at

4 large bell peppers (capsicums)
1 small onion
4 garlic cloves
¾oz (25g) butter
7oz (200g) couscous
1 cube vegetable stock
1 cup (8¾fl oz/250ml) hot water
13oz (400g) corn
3½oz (100g) cheddar or Parmesan cheese
chipotle (smoked chili pepper) according to taste
1 batch tomato sauce *(see page 28)*

home? No problem. You can substitute with jalapeño or finely chopped spicy sausage if you're not intent on keeping this a vegetarian dish). Stuff the peppers with the couscous, top with remaining cheese, add the lids, place in an ovenproof dish and bake for about 30 minutes or until you can see black bubbles start to form on the pepper lids.

24 Baked bell peppers (capsicum) *with toasted couscous*

26 Bolognese, Tomato Sauce, Italian veal ragu *with lemon and thyme*

Spaghetti with meat sauce, also known by its fancier name of *Spaghetti Bolognese*, is every households' culinary equivalent of the *missionary*; a regularly recurring feature of everyday life which the majority of the adult population has, to some extent, come to master and appreciate. Over time, however, some individuals may ask themselves if the basic concept could possibly be *developed*, *refined* or just *varied* a little. To this I can only reply: Did you ever try it with a carrot?

Bolognese

Chop the onion finely and the garlic even finer. Cook with olive oil in frying pan over medium heat, then add the ground beef and fry thoroughly.

While the meat and onions are cooking, grate the carrots and celeriac on the fine side of a shredder. Puree the tomatoes in a blender or use a rod mixer (or you can simply squash them with your hand). Add carrots and celeriac and let simmer for a few minutes. Add tomatoes, honey, tomato puree and fish sauce.

1 large onion
3 garlic cloves
13oz (400g) ground beef
2 carrots
¼ celeriac
1 can whole tomatoes
1 tablespoon honey
1 tablespoon tomato puree
1-2 tablespoon Asian fish sauce
1 lemon

Wash the lemon, then grate, ever so gently, the zest (the thin yellow part of the peel) and squeeze out the lemon juice. Add zest and juice according to taste. Let simmer for about 10 minutes. Taste with salt and freshly ground black pepper.

Serve with al dente spaghetti and grated Parmesan cheese.

Tomato sauce

Use a somewhat larger pot. Chop the garlic finely and cook in oil over medium heat. Just as it starts to turn golden, add the tomatoes. Use a rod mixer to mix smoothly. Add honey, taste with salt and freshly ground black pepper.

5 garlic cloves
2 cans whole tomatoes
2 teaspoon honey
about ½ tablespoon balsamic vinegar

Add the balsamic vinegar little by little, carefully tasting your way as different brands vary in concentration.

Let simmer for a few minutes, then serve.

From a culinary point of view, Rome ought to be one of the most interesting capitals in the world. The problem is finding the authentic Roman kitchen before you're lured into one of the city's many tourist traps where you have to make your way through hoards of Germans in Birkenstocks, ruffling their maps and talking in very loud voices. Theoretically, the solution could be identifying the very spot where Rome's policemen eat their dinners.
You could spend many, many hours in a vain search for the place where *Il Carabiniere* tuck in *Bollito Misto*. Or you could walk into that trattoria that looks so depressing, what with the fluorescent lamps and all, and order their divine veal ragu with lemon and thyme. Or you could pack up your bags, take the plane home and cook it yourself.

Italian veal ragu *with lemon and thyme*

Peel the garlic cloves and chop them finely, then fry in a little bit of olive oil. Lower the heat, add the ground veal and fry thoroughly. Mash the tomatoes with a rod mixer or with your hand and add those.

Wash the lemons and grate the zest with a light and gentle hand (just the yellow part, no pith). Add the zest of both lemons but juice from only one to the sauce.

5 garlic cloves
13oz (400g) finely ground veal
2 tins whole or crushed tomatoes
2 lemons
1 tablespoon tomato paste
white pepper
1 pot fresh thyme

Let the sauce simmer until it thickens a bit, then add tomato paste, white pepper, salt and perhaps a teaspoon of sugar (skip the sugar if the tomatoes are sweet). Tear the leaves off the thyme and add those too.

Serve with freshly cooked pasta and loads of Parmesan cheese.

Every liberating exercise comes with a certain amount of risk. This is also true for *the crushing of lemongrass*, an undertaking that gives the chicken skewers in this recipe a fine, somewhat perfumed citrus taste.

Use a blunt object that you feel comfortable with (a hammer, a frozen leg of lamb, your dad's old walking shoe or whatever you reach for when you're being violent). Place one stick of lemongrass at a time on a stable, sturdy surface. Breathe slowly, inhale through your nose, exhale through your mouth, set your mind free and POUND, POUND, POUND, until the grass shatters to the core.

I strongly encourage you to multiply the recipe, to avoid having to interrupt the therapeutic pounding simply because you're done just as old injustices begin to come undone from the silt of your soul.

And since neither of us know yet what you're walking around with inside —be sure to lock up all your large knives before you get going.

Chicken *on lemongrass skewers*

Preheat the oven to 340°F (175°C/Gas Mark 4). In a food processor, chop the chicken into a coarse mince. Grate the ginger finely, cup it in your hand and squeeze the juice into a bowl (discard the remaining, dry ginger). Combine chicken meat, ginger juice, egg, salt and as much breadcrumbs as you need for the mince to stick together.

Pound the thicker end of each lemongrass stick until it shreds. Pour a few drops of oil into the palms of your hands and pick up enough of the meat mixture to shape an oval ball, then press this onto the lemongrass and squeeze so that it sticks. Repeat with the rest of the meat mixture, then roll the skewers in breadcrumbs.

16oz (500g) chicken
   (thigh fillet)
1 knob ginger,
   the size of
   a large thumb
1 egg
½ teaspoon salty
   breadcrumbs,
   preferably Panko,
   a Japanese variety
approx. 16 sticks of
   lemongrass
3½oz (100g) peanuts
2 tablespoons sesame
   seeds
lime

Heat a ½-inch (1cm) thick layer of oil in a frying pan. Fry the skewers until golden all over. Transfer to an oven dish and cook until done, about 20 minutes.

Crush the peanuts. Roast the sesame seeds in a dry frying pan. Sprinkle the skewers with seeds and nuts. Serve with lime wedges and the melon salad on *page 114*.

TIE-BREAKER NUMBER 1:

It's an early winter morning and you have just woken up next to someone who is, let's be honest, a little too good for you. What do you do?

A) Sneak out of bed, heading straight for the bathroom. Start washing up with soap and water, proceeding to enhance yourself with the help of toothpaste, eye drops, concealer, lipstick, razor, Neti pot, padded undies and musk oil.

B) Sneak out of bed, and head straight for the stove.

Banana pancakes *with tropical fruit*

Whisk together egg, coconut milk, flour, sugar and salt. Slice the bananas and add them to the batter. Heat a little butter in a frying pan and fry small pancakes—keep fried pancakes warm in the oven at 300°F (150°C/Gas Mark 2) while you fry up the rest of the batter.

Serve with thinly sliced pineapple and/or mango, roasted sesame seeds, pistachios or cashew nuts, runny honey or maple syrup, thick Greek-style yogurt or vanilla ice cream.

1 egg
1 can of coconut
  milk
5oz (150g) plain
  flour
2 tablespoons sugar
¼ teaspoon salt
2 bananas
butter for frying

36 Lasagne *with hazelnut pesto, aubergine and portabella*

Whenever I make lasagne, I have this recurring thought: that lasagne was originally introduced not as a dish but as a form of therapy originating from one the American-Austrian sexologist Wilhelm Reich's disciples. My theory is that the disciple regarded lasagne as an instrumental device in letting the patient confront his inner stress as dinner is never, never ready.

Lasagne demands a lot; time, simultaneous capacity and effort, three ingredients the majority of us find it hard to mobilise at any given moment. And yet, people love lasagne. Think about why the next time you stand there, next to a bubbling bechamel as you simultaneously fry aubergine (eggplant) and portabella into a garlic-scented mash and mix parsley with nuts and ricotta. Is it because the lasagne is an internationally acclaimed alternative to the ever-popular Swedish sandwich layer cake? Or is it because a lasagne has the ability to give you that rare sense of satisfaction as you *for once* succeed in arranging a few of all the messy elements in life between tidy sheets of pasta?

Lasagne *with hazelnut pesto, aubergine and portabella*

Preheat the oven to 400°F (200°C/Gas Mark 6). In a blender or mixer, mix nuts, parsley, egg, salt, pepper and 13oz (400g) of the ricotta into a smooth pesto. Set aside.

Clean, trim and dice mushrooms and aubergines (eggplant) finely. Slice the garlic finely. Fry to a lovely soft mash in as much butter or olive oil as the situation calls for. Season with salt and pepper. Make a bechamel from the recipe in this book and once it's done, thicken it even more with the remaining ricotta cheese.

Smear a thin layer of the pesto all over the bottom of an ovenproof dish and cover with a layer of lasagne sheets. Spread a layer of aubergine mash on top and cover with a thin layer of bechamel. Repeat until all filling and all lasagne sheets have been used. Garnish with sliced cherry tomatoes and squeeze some lemon over it all and sprinkle with flake salt, then drizzle a little, little bit of olive oil over the whole thing.

Cook in oven for about 45 minutes.

7oz (200g) roasted hazelnuts (peeled)
32oz (1kg) flat-leaved parsley, just the leaves
1 egg
1 teaspoon salt
1 teaspoon freshly ground black pepper
16oz (500g) ricotta cheese
4 portabella mushrooms
2 small aubergines (eggplants)
4 garlic cloves
2 batches bechamel *(see page 9)*
16oz (500g) fresh lasagne sheets
27oz (800g) cherry tomatoes
½ lemon

Of all the known ways of limiting your food intake, I can only really sympathise with vegetarianism. Nevertheless, I have never succeeded in understanding why its most extreme perpetrators persist in throwing stones during G20 meetings, decorating themselves with exotic tattoos and wearing their hair in the shape of slim sausages. If the message to the rest of us is *that we should eat less meat* (a both true, wise and relevant demand), shouldn't there be a better, nicer and more effective way to communicate? Perhaps we could all sit down with a bowl of soup and simply *talk* instead?

Striped carrot soup *with vanilla, lemon and cinnamon*

Peel and cut the carrots into chunks, put in pot together with cinnamon stick and pour in enough water to cover the carrots and then a tiny bit more.

Cook the carrots until they are nice and soft. Fish out the cinnamon stick and discard. Mix the carrots (and the water you cooked them in) into a puree. Add butter and vanilla, dilute with water until the soup has the texture you think an ideal soup should have. Season with salt and keep the soup warm. Wash the lemon and grate the zest with a light and gentle hand (just the yellow part, no pith).

Mix together carrot juice, maple syrup, the zest from the entire lemon but only half of the

32oz (1kg) organic
  carrots
1 cinnamon stick
1¾oz (50g) butter
½ teaspoon vanilla
  powder (powdered
  vanilla beans, found
  among baking
  supplies)
1 lemon
7fl oz (200ml) freshly
  squeezed carrot
  juice
1½ tablespoons
  maple syrup

juice from the same. Pour into the hot soup and stir carefully one time around the soup so that the two carrot soups blend just a little but not completely.

Ladle into soup bowls and serve.

Everyday life is not always compatible with the orthodox kind of moussaka, especially not those nights when you have one child on your hip; another hugging your leg and it's already half past six before you've grated that darn onion. Sure, one can focus on the *Vision* and refuse any deviation from the original *Grand Idea* and the *Great Plan* to realise one's dream. That's what Donald Trump does, no matter if someone cries and hits him with a comic book while he whips up a cheese sauce, blow-dries his hair or plans a new shopping mall.

However, the overwhelming majority of us are not Donald Trump. So let me introduce you to a different kind of moussaka; a quicker, easier and really delicious kind.

Moussaka *with red pesto and feta cheese*

Preheat the oven to 440°F (225°C/Gas Mark 7) grill.

Grate the onion coarsely, the garlic finely and combine with ground lamb, pesto, cinnamon and drained, mashed artichoke hearts. Season with salt and pepper and mix well (you're best off using your own clean hands for this task).

Shred the aubergines (eggplants) and peeled potatoes on the coarse side of a box grater, season with salt and squeeze the lemon over it all.

Layer the meat mix with the shredded vegetables in an ovenproof dish. Top with cherry tomatoes and diced feta cheese.

Cook for about 40 minutes and serve with a crispy green salad.

2 onions
3 garlic cloves
13oz (400g) ground lamb
1 jar (7oz/200g) red pesto
½ teaspoon ground cinnamon
1 can artichoke hearts
2 small aubergines (eggplants)
4 potatoes
½ lemon
16oz (500g) cherry tomatoes on the vine
8oz (250g) feta cheese, authentic Greek

"*And please, don't make them pancakes for dinner again*," was the last thing our mum would tell Dad on days when she would be working late. "*No pancakes, OK*," Dad replied, and then made us waffles instead.

Exactly why some women feel inadequate as parents when they serve pancakes for dinner is a mystery to me. But I do know that carrots and parsnips are chockfull of great fibres and vitamins and that maple syrup and warm goat's cheese do wonders when cooking root vegetables.

If you fall into the category of really respectable and responsible parents you may cut any associations to irresponsible pancakes by calling this an *everyday root vegetable dish*. Just don't let the children hear it.

Root vegetable pancake *with goat's cheese and maple syrup*

Preheat the oven to 440°F (225°C/Gas Mark 7) grill.

Whisk the eggs. Add salt and half of the milk; add the flour and the rest of the milk while whisking. Peel and grate the root vegetables and stir into the batter. Line a roasting pan with baking paper, pour the batter in and bake for about 20 minutes or until the pancake looks done.

Remove from oven, add the goat's cheese in bits or thin slices, drizzle with

3 eggs
2 teaspoons salt
17fl oz (500ml) milk
10oz (300g) spelt or wheat flour
2 carrots
1 parsnip
5oz (150g) soft goat's cheese
maple syrup

maple syrup then bring the whole shebang back into the oven, for about 2 minutes, to give the cheese time to get a little warm but not enough to melt.

Serve with a salad, perhaps very, very finely shredded point cabbage or regular cabbage quickly fried in a little oil before mixing it with a bit of toasted coconut flakes and sultanas or dried, shredded apricots.

Few foods struggle with a greater image problem than lentils. Sensitive souls can barely read the words *lentil soup* before they suffer brain meltdown from an overload of images of Indian beaches invaded by white girls in tank tops and turbans, doing yoga. At night, these ladies sit inside their tents, stirring their soups with wooden ladles in poorly washed pots. There's a strong smell of dirty wool, scalp and incense.

As soon as dinner is ready, hoards of young men with guitars climb in through the tent opening. The girls dispense splats of thick lentil porridge in a few bowls. The lads fuss a little with their bracelets and yawn. And so on.

And yes, lentils are certainly both inexpensive and popular in India. But (and any hedonist silver fox who recently sold his house in the suburbs and has at least one gourmet trip to Tuscany on his conscience will tell you this): lentils are also very *Italian*.

And delicious.

Green lentils *with tomatoes*

Take out a rather large pot and pour lots of water into it, which you bring to a boil. Add the lentils, remove from the heat and cover with a lid. Let the lentils swell for about 30 minutes. Then simmer over low heat for about 15 minutes.

Get another pot out. Crush the fennel seeds in a mortar, then fry them in the pot with some olive oil until your entire kitchen smells of liquorice.

Add tomatoes, water, garlic puree, honey, balsamic vinegar and drained lentils. Season with salt and freshly ground pepper and serve with fried salsiccia.

7oz (200g) green
   lentils, dried
1½ teaspoons fennel
   seeds
1 can cherry tomatoes
2¾fl oz (100ml) water
1 tablespoon garlic
   puree *(see page 10)*
1 tablespoon honey
½ tablespoon balsamic
   vinegar
4 salsiccia sausages

If there's any kind of humour that will be around till the end of time, it's bound to be skilful impersonations of immensely famous people. Michael Caine is a rewarding subject as well as Sir David Attenborough and Sean Connery. However, skilful imitation does require lots of skill. Should this quality be missing, it is better to refrain from humour altogether, or—if you have to make fun of something—go for easier targets, like mimicking country bumpkins. You know the kind. Fennel, for instance.

Faux fennel *to be served with fried salsiccia*

Trim the cabbage from any sad, limp leaves, cut away and discard the tough base, then shred the cabbage as finely as you possibly can. Chop the onion finely. Crush fennel seeds and anise in a mortar. Sweat onion, fennel seeds and anise in butter or oil until the onion is translucent.

Wash the lemon and grate the zest with a light and gentle hand (just the yellow part, no pith). Add zest, cabbage, syrup or sugar and creme fraiche to the onion fry. Season with salt and freshly ground black pepper. Serve with fried salsiccia.

1 small head pointed cabbage
1 onion
1 teaspoon fennel seeds
1 teaspoon anise
1 lemon
1 tablespoon syrup or sugar
7fl oz (200ml) creme fraiche
4 (raw) salsiccia sausages

Faux fennel *to be served with fried salsiccia* **49**

50 Corn pancakes *with shrimp and avocado*

Martin Luther, reformer of the Christian faith and among other things known for calling the reigning pope *The Antichrist*, decided, at the age of 42, to put an end to his bachelor days and to exchange his long nights of lonely work at the work desk for twosome meetings between the sheets with a twenty years younger nun who was smuggled out of her cloister in a poorly cleaned herring barrel.

Personally, I find this story immensely inspiring. It is proof that no one, not even *stern old men in funny hats*, should have to keep living like they always have. Do you for instance think that pancakes should always be served with maple syrup simply because that's how they've always been eaten in your home?

It's time for you to reconsider.

Corn pancakes *with shrimp and avocado*

Defrost the shrimp, shell them and chop coarsely. If using frozen corn, rinse it with a little water straight from the tap to let it thaw a little. Whisk the eggs with half of the coconut milk.

Add flour and salt and whisk until batter is free of lumps. Add remaining coconut milk and stir in corn and shrimp. If you have the time, let the batter sit for a little while.

Put some butter in a frying pan and fry small pancakes over medium heat (you can keep fried pancakes warm in the oven at 300°F (150°C/Gas Mark 2) while you fry up the rest of the batter). Serve with fixings.

16oz (500g) frozen
   shrimp with shells
   (cooked)
16oz (500g) sweet corn
2 eggs
2 tins coconut milk
10oz (300g) flour
1 teaspoon salt

Fixings
2 avocados
1 pot coriander
lime
sour cream
green Tabasco

Some simply don't photograph well. Those of us who have spent decades in front of a mirror to finally find a working photo face by flexing our features in a muscular smile as we simultaneously lift our eyebrows, push our tongues way up in the roof of the mouth while thinking of a petite French apple often have difficulty in accepting this fact.

We keep working: how about testing a different angle? *Doesn't work.* What about spicing things up with saffron? *Nope.* Placing a superfluous lime wedge somewhere? *No.* How about some attractive bread then? *I told you it wouldn't work.* Top it off with a fistful of raisins? *May I PLEASE BE EXCUSED NOW?*

But come on. It's not the end of the world if you don't photograph well, I can hear you mumble. That's easy for you to say. You're not a recipe.

Potato curry *with saffron and spinach*

Peel and dice the potatoes. Pour some oil into a frying pan and fry the potatoes until it takes on a beautiful, slightly golden colour. Remove from heat and set aside.

Finely chop the garlic, halve and slice the onion finely, then sweat the garlic and onion in a little olive oil until translucent. Add cumin, coriander and saffron and let fry for a minute while stirring.

Add rinsed, drained chickpeas, fried potatoes, coconut milk and sugar. Cover and let simmer for about 15 minutes or until the potatoes are tender. Taste and season with salt (start with ½ teaspoon) and juice from one lime.

While waiting for the potatoes to soften, dice the halloumi and fry in a hot pan in some oil until it takes on a beautiful colour. Add the spinach to the curry, heat gently and serve with fried halloumi, sultanas and the extra lime.

4 large potatoes of
  a nice, firm variety
2 garlic cloves
2 onions
1 teaspoon cumin,
  ground
½ teaspoon coriander,
  ground
½g saffron
1 tin of chickpeas
1 tin coconut milk
1 teaspoon sugar
1 lime + 1 more lime
  for serving
7oz (200g) halloumi
  cheese
7oz (200g) fresh spinach
3½oz (100g) sultanas

A friend of mine was once invited to a wolf hunt in Siberia. Since he wasn't familiar with the local cuisine, he packed his backpacking stove and filled one of his boots with pasta. *The first* night, he was served a tough, incredibly sad elk muzzle in unsalted broth. *The second*, *third* and *fourth* night too. The Siberian cold was omnipresent. The Siberian wolf was nowhere to be found. As the weekend approached, the host announced that there would be pizza on Friday. The guest, weary of muzzle and secret nightly cooking of pasta, looked forward to the pizza until it was ceremoniously placed on the table: A bream with scales, fins and head still intact crowning an incredibly thick disk of dough, all cut in four even pieces. It was a bream pizza. There are people who say that pasta is not good for you. Perhaps they are right. *But there are times when pasta can save your life.*

Open lasagne *with spinach, ricotta and almond pesto*

Serves 2 people

Roast the almonds properly in a dry frying pan, then crush them in a mortar, mill or food processor. Set aside. Melt the butter. Separate the clear butter from the cloudy residue. Discard the latter and let the clarified butter bubble for a minute over low heat until a wonderful toffee aroma spreads in your kitchen. Wash the lemon and grate the zest with a light and gentle hand (just the yellow part, no pith). Add crushed almonds, zest and honey to the butter and stir. Season with salt and a few drops of lemon juice. Keep warm.

In a large pot, bring a generous amount of salted water to a boil (this is to be used for the lasagne sheets). Chop the onion finely and the garlic even finer, sweat in butter or olive oil until translucent.

1¾oz (50g) almonds
¾oz (25g) butter
1 lemon
½ teaspoon honey
1 large onion
1 garlic clove
8oz (250g) wood
  mushrooms or
  portabella
4 slices of Serrano ham
  (if you'd like, not
  necessary)
7oz (200g) fresh
  spinach
2 fresh lasagne sheets,
  average size
8oz (250g) ricotta
  cheese

Slice the mushrooms finely, shred the ham and fold into the fried onions.

Fry until the mushroom takes on a little colour. Add the spinach and keep frying until it has performed its magic shrinking act. Season with salt and be generous with freshly ground black pepper.

Cook the lasagne sheets al dente, fish them out of the water with a perforated ladle and place one each on two plates. Distribute half of the spinach filling on one end of each lasagne sheet, top with a hearty dollop of ricotta cheese and fold over the rest of the pasta (take a look at the picture on the next page if you're getting confused—this is much less complicated than it sounds). Spoon warm almond pesto over your creation and serve immediately.

Church representatives love to talk about how Jesus and his disciples managed to feed all of five thousand people with the help of nothing more than two fish and five loaves of bread. But what is rarely mentioned is that when everybody had had their share and was supposedly full, there were *no less than twelve baskets* left, filled with bread—and fish leftovers. It says so in the Bible, promise. Look it up if you don't believe me. I'm not trying to trump Jesus, but imagine, just imagine that He'd spiffed up his dish with a few simple sides such as avocado, lemon, dill and mayonnaise?

Just saying, would there have been any *leftovers* if He had?

Fish burgers

In a food processor, chop fish into a coarse mince. Mash the potatoes with a fork. Combine breadcrumbs, egg, potatoes and fish, season with salt and pepper and shape into four generous patties. Fry in butter, about 3 minutes on each side.

Mash or slice the avocado. Chop the dill finely. Combine dill, mayonnaise and lemon juice.

Heat the buns in the oven or fry them nice and golden in butter. Place lettuce leaves and avocado on the bottom part of the buns; put the fish patties on top and crown with the dill mayonnaise. Serve with wedge potatoes and pickles.

10oz (300g) fish fillet
3 boiled potatoes, peeled
1¾oz (50g) breadcrumbs, preferably Panko, a Japanese variety
1 egg
2 avocados
1 pot dill
1¾fl oz (50ml) mayonnaise
½ lemon
4 buns, halved
1 pot of bag crispy salad

Fennel risotto *to be served with grilled fish*

The great majority of people who have ever tried to write anything about fennel have felt the need to mention that fennel was considered a *potent aphrodisiac* in ancient Greece. Considered? Either fennel was really:

A) A potent aphrodisiac in ancient Greece,

OR this view merely represents

B) Something that the average ancient Greek person had misunderstood, most likely because it must have been as impossible then as it is now to regard the fennel without noticing how youthfully pert, potent and perky it seems.

But wouldn't it be more relevant to question the need for sexually stimulating aids during antiquity? After all, this was long before contemporary erotic turn-offs such as *Champions League*, *iPhone* and arguing over whose turn it is to *change the baby's nappy*. Back then, people walked around naked, carrying a maximum of a small discus, no one fell asleep on the couch once the kids were finally sleeping, and the sun was always shining. People had too much time to ponder non-essential matters in ancient Greece.

That is my opinion. And this is my idea of a really great risotto.

Fennel risotto *to be served with grilled fish*

Cut away and discard the tough base of the root and side shoots from the fennel bulbs, but keep the cute little sprigs. Cut in large chunks, place in pit and pour over just enough water to cover. Let the fennel simmer under lid until soft.

Grind the fennel seeds in a mortar and add them to the pot to let them cook with the fresh fennel for a few minutes. Pour the contents of the pot (fennel, water and all) together with the sprigs into a food processor or blender and mix into a smooth puree.

Wash the lemon and grate the zest with a light and gentle hand (just the yellow part, no pith). Pour a generous amount into a thick-bottomed pot and fry zest, finely chopped shallots and garlic over low heat for a few minutes. Add the rice and let fry while stirring—use a wooden ladle and make sure

2 fennel bulbs
2 teaspoons fennel seeds
1 lemon
2 shallots
2 garlic cloves
13oz (400g) risotto rice
7fl oz (200ml) white wine
17fl oz (500ml chicken stock (stock cube + water)
7fl oz (200ml) creme fraiche
1 pot fresh French tarragon

nothing gets burned along the way. Add the wine and let it settle in and evaporate while stirring continuously. If you need to, turn the heat up—you want to hear a bubbling, fizzling sound as soon as you add any liquid.

Meanwhile, heat the stock in a different pot. Add one ladle of hot stock at the time and let it vanish into the risotto before you add another. Keep stirring! Making a risotto should be a continuous, slightly fatiguing stirring exercise until it is put on the table.

Once the rice starts to get the desirable texture—a rich and creamy exterior with a somewhat al dente core—add the fennel puree. Taste and season with freshly ground black pepper and lemon juice. Right before serving, add creme fraiche and finely chopped tarragon.

Serve with salad and grilled fish.

Water steam is a *gas*. It is not, contrary to what many people believe, a humid kind of hot air primarily found in tropical countries where its top priority is to ruin people's hairstyles. When vapour hits a cool surface *the same amount of energy is released in the shape of heat as was lost during the transformation of water into steam*.

That's the reason why steaming is such a great and effective method of cooking compared to a convection oven at the same temperature. And if you've ever taken a sauna and marvelled at how well you could take the heat until that thick-skinned person came in, pouring water on the aggregate…well now you know.

Steamed fish *with lime leaves and lemongrass*

Did I mention this recipe also requires a bamboo steamer? No? Well, I'm mentioning it now.

Salt the fish fillets lightly on both sides. Pound the lemongrass sticks with a blunt object until you can divide grass into long shreds. Cut across the lime leaves a few times. Arrange the lemongrass and lime leaves in the bottom of the steamer so that

20oz (600g) fish fillets
  (suitable fish
  varieties are hoki,
  pikeperch or perch)
4 lemongrass sticks
1 bunch fresh lime
  leaves
1 lime

it's almost covered. Put the fish fillets on top together with the lime, cut in wedges. Cover with the lid and place the steamer on top of a pot with boiling water. Steam until the fish meat divides along its natural sections when light pressure is applied.

Squeeze lime over the fish and serve, perhaps with the coconut rice on *page 118* and any of the salads on *pages 68* or *114*.

I often wonder why people don't buy minced chicken. As far as I know, almost no one has turned blind, leper or been burnt at the stake after having purchased, cooked or eaten minced chicken. Quite on the contrary, this is a versatile minced meat variety well worth its money.

Yes, I agree there may be something anaemic about this pink outsider in the meat counter, and *no*, it will never win any awards due to its personality or exciting looks *but that's the point*! Minced chicken meat is a quiet pragmatist; the perfect companion for colourful individuals such as ginger, chilli, lime leaves and coriander.

Minced chicken meat never steals the show, never gets too loud or overwhelming. No, minced chicken meat stays in the background but gets the job done. The truth is that minced chicken meat has many of the qualities that characterises a great leader, qualities often lacking in the people that head many of today's important young media companies. And *yes*, you're right, I may have spent too much time thinking about minced chicken meat.

Asian chicken salad *with chilli and lime leaves*

Chop the garlic cloves finely and let fry for a minute, add the minced chicken meat and fry through.

Shred the ginger finely, then cup the ginger with your hand and squeeze out the juice into a small bowl. (Discard the dry ginger fibre ball that remains when you are done juicing). De-seed and finely slice the chillies.

Mix ginger juice, chilli, fish sauce, sugar and the juice from one lime. Add the juice mix into the chicken while stirring. Shred the lime leaves and add those too. Let simmer over low heat. Season with fish sauce and lime juice.

Trim the lettuce of limp or ugly leaves, then tear off the remaining leaves and arrange as bowls on a large plate. Chop the coriander (the stems too) and the nuts.

Slice the snow peas lengthwise. Fill the lettuce leaves with the chicken meat and top with sliced snow peas, chopped nuts and coriander and serve immediately.

5 garlic cloves
13oz (400g) minced chicken meat
1 thumb-sized knob ginger
2–3 red chillies
2 tablespoons Asian fish sauce
1 tablespoon brown sugar
2 limes
6 lime leaves
2 heads iceberg lettuce (pick light ones)
1 pot fresh coriander
3½oz (100g) peanuts or roasted cashew nuts
3½oz (100g) snow peas

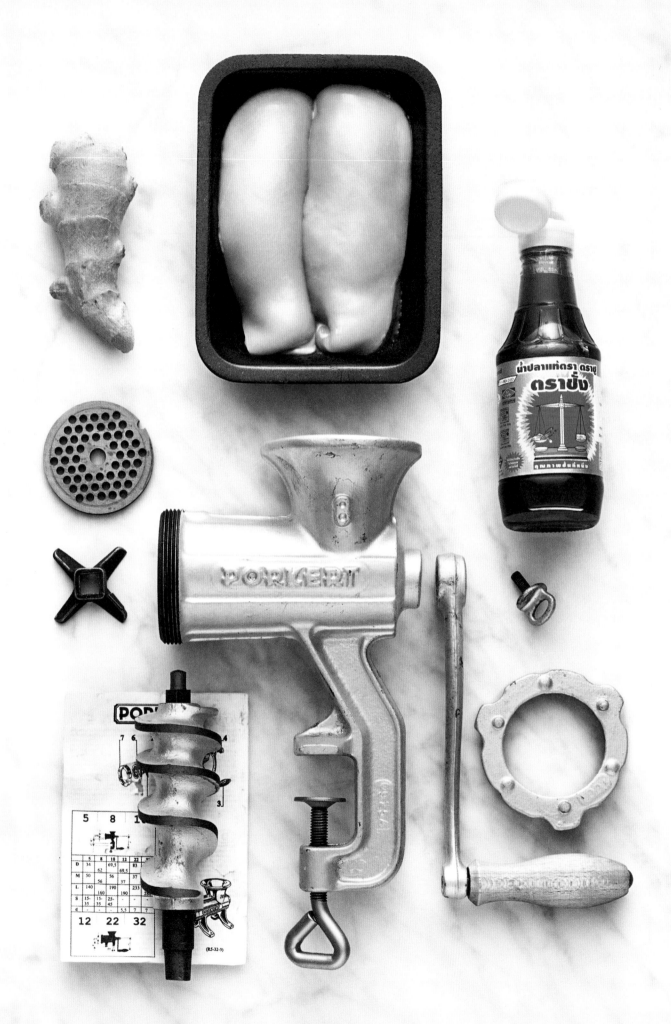

When watermelon is perfect—crunchy, juicy and sweet. It is a delicacy. And when it is crumbly, foam rubber-dry and grainy, it is a very sad vegetarian equivalent of haggis.

According to experts, you should knock on the melon and judge the contents before you've purchased, carried home and opened the fruit. But what sound should you listen for as you knock? *Pock-pock? Cong-chong? Klonk-klonk?* If you're one of those lucky people who can easily distinguish the tchi-tchi-tcha-tcha-sortitooo of the chaffinch from the wheep-wheep-chittichittichiittichitta of the chiffchaff , *pock pock* and *chong chong* are probably excellent guidance.

Personally, however, I find this method to be about as reliable as kicking the tyres to make sure you're not being fooled when buying a used car.

Watermelon salad *with fennel and pomegranate*

Cut the melon in thick slices, then dice the red flesh into large cubes. Remove the base of the root and the tough shoots from the fennel and slice the rest really thin (a Mandolin shredder is great for this kind of slicing).

De-seed the pomegranate. Shred the basil. Shred the ginger finely on a grater, press ginger juice into a bowl by using your hand and discard ginger once you are done.

1 small watermelon
1 fennel bulb
1 pomegranate
1 pot Thai basil
1 thumb-sized knob ginger
3 limes
3 tablespoons olive oil
1 tablespoon sugar
pinch of salt

Mix pressed lime, ginger juice, olive oil, sugar and salt, and stir until sugar is fully dissolved. Arrange the fruit and fennel on a plate, drizzle dressing over it all and top with Thai basil.

Watermelon salad *with fennel and pomegranate* 69

Every June, Swedish men feel their season has begun. Burnt by the sun, potbellied and wonderfully carefree, they abandon all normal decency and do what only Swedish men do—meet the summer bare-chested. Walking through the town. In the local store. Behind the wheel. On the bus. Happily and unabashed, as if it was a legal right to treat all fellow humans to a generous sight of one's more or less well-fed flesh.

It's easy to make analogies between the Swedish male and Swedish food. Despite the fact Swedish men have, for decades, tried to export the naked upper body to various charter destinations, the behaviour has remained a Swedish phenomenon. And despite the fact Swedish food has time and time again been launched as something exotic and exciting, it has never really had any success beyond the Swedish borders. "Nasty old meat," the rest of the world mutters, "Let those uncivilised Swedes keep it to themselves."

Couscous salad *with strawberries and goat's cheese*

Melt the butter in a saucepan, add uncooked couscous and keep stirring until the grains take on a slightly golden colour. Pour over the hot, salted water; remove from the heat, cover and let swell for a few minutes.

Cut fruit, berries and vegetables into chunks. Whisk together olive oil, lemon juice and sugar, and season with a pinch of salt and freshly ground pepper. Make the salad by arranging the drained couscous, fruit, berries, vegetables, fresh mint, rocket and soft goat's cheese (broken into smaller pieces) and dressing as nicely as you can.

2 tablespoons butter
8oz (250g) couscous
12fl oz (350ml)
    piping hot water
    + ¼ teaspoon salt
1 small melon, any
    variety you like
1 litre fresh
    strawberries
2 avocados
½ cucumber
2½oz (75g) snow peas
1¾fl oz (50 ml) olive oil

½ lemon, squeezed
1 teaspoon sugar
1 pot fresh mint
2½oz (75g) rocket salad
5oz (150g) soft
    goat's cheese

Monday

Thursday

Tuesday

Friday

So watermelon might not be the most filling inhabitant of the food universe. ON THE OTHER HAND, nothing stops you from stopping by your local Indian later tonight. Or from standing by the sink, eating a whole pan of potato gratin, in the middle of the night.

Watermelon
with ouzo and feta cheese

Cut the melon in chunks or shape melon balls with the help of a spoon. Put in a bowl, pour the ouzo over, stir carefully and let stand in a cool place for at least an hour.

Dice the feta, shred the mint leaves and mix with the melon.

½ watermelon
2¾fl oz (100ml) ouzo
8oz (250g) feta cheese, authentic Greek
1 pot fresh mint

The trouble with salads is often their alarming *lack of excitement*, a fact that has everything to do with low temperatures, high water content and an annoyingly flimsy personality. Despite being sprinkled with generous amounts of dressing, many salads still squeak as you chew—and no matter how you chew your salad, there is never any satisfactory contact with the inside of your mouth.

To add to the misery, many salads are boring to prepare, unless you're wildly entertained by chopping vegetables into average sized chunks. Which only happens during the five minutes following the purchase of a new, slightly too expensive knife.

That's why I feel so happy about this salad, which is completely different. It's a *hot, original salad* chockfull of controversial ingredients such as raw onion, garlic, fish sauce and brined chicken.

Still too little drama for you? Then try serving this dish to anyone who dislikes coriander.

Thai cucumber salad *with brined chicken*

Trim the chicken fillets. Whisk together the brine ingredients and stir until sugar and salt have dissolved completely. Put the chicken into the brine and leave in a cool place for at least 2 hours, longer if possible.

Once brined, let brined chicken fillets simmer in water or chicken stock for roughly 10 minutes. Remove from heat, pour the liquid away and cover and put aside to chill.

Slice the onion very, very finely and then put the sliced onion in a bowl with ice-cold water. Shave the cucumber lengthwise using a Mandolin shredder or potato peeler. Finely chop the garlic and chilli. Chop the coriander—the entire plant, stems and all.

Combine fish sauce, sugar, squeezed lime juice and lemon, and whisk until the sugar has dissolved. Slice the chicken thinly. Drain the onion in colander.

Chicken:
2–3 chicken fillets
35fl oz (1 litre) water
1¾oz (50g) salt
2 tablespoons sugar

Salad:
2 onions
2 thin cucumbers, organic if possible
4 garlic cloves
2 red chillies
2 pots coriander
2 tablespoons fish sauce
2 tablespoons sugar
2 limes
½ lemon
cooked rice

In a bowl, combine onion, cucumber, garlic, chilli, coriander and chicken, and pour the dressing over it all.

Serve with freshly cooked rice.

Tip:
If you're too short on time to brine the chicken yourself, take the easy route by buying a ready grilled chicken and simply remove the skin.

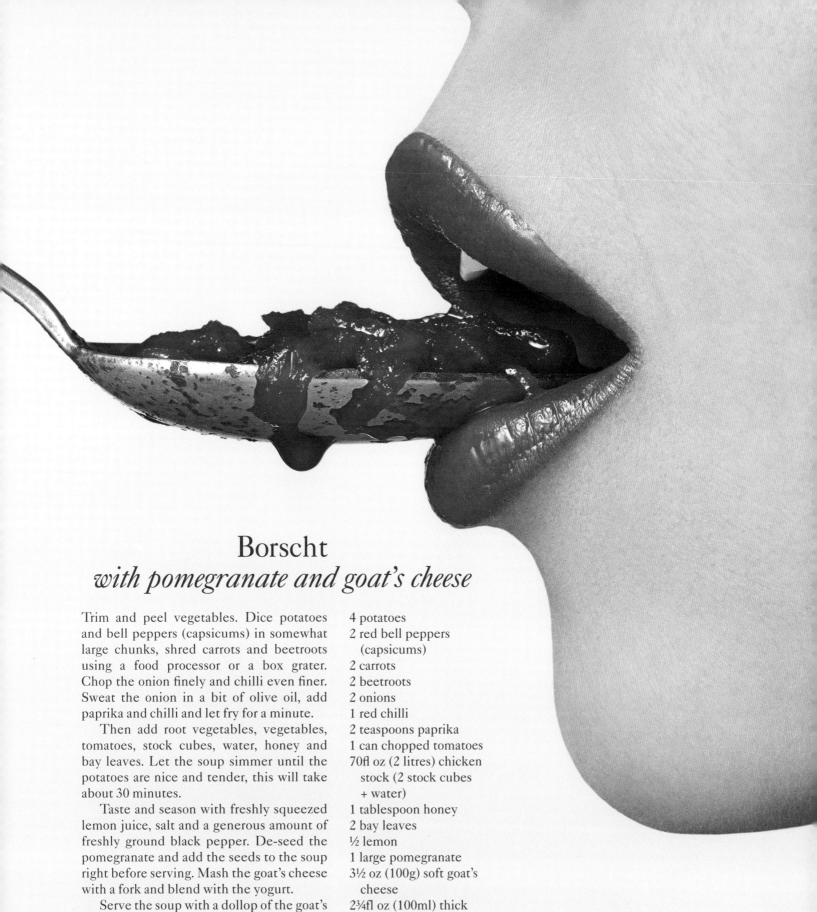

Borscht
with pomegranate and goat's cheese

Trim and peel vegetables. Dice potatoes and bell peppers (capsicums) in somewhat large chunks, shred carrots and beetroots using a food processor or a box grater. Chop the onion finely and chilli even finer. Sweat the onion in a bit of olive oil, add paprika and chilli and let fry for a minute.

Then add root vegetables, vegetables, tomatoes, stock cubes, water, honey and bay leaves. Let the soup simmer until the potatoes are nice and tender, this will take about 30 minutes.

Taste and season with freshly squeezed lemon juice, salt and a generous amount of freshly ground black pepper. De-seed the pomegranate and add the seeds to the soup right before serving. Mash the goat's cheese with a fork and blend with the yogurt.

Serve the soup with a dollop of the goat's cheese yogurt mix and perhaps the soft flatbreads on *page 9*.

4 potatoes
2 red bell peppers (capsicums)
2 carrots
2 beetroots
2 onions
1 red chilli
2 teaspoons paprika
1 can chopped tomatoes
70fl oz (2 litres) chicken stock (2 stock cubes + water)
1 tablespoon honey
2 bay leaves
½ lemon
1 large pomegranate
3½ oz (100g) soft goat's cheese
2¾fl oz (100ml) thick Greek-style cooking yogurt (10 per cent fat)

78 Savoy cabbage rolls *with lamb and chanterelles*

You could argue that *Savoy cabbage* is the vegetable equivalent of *Iggy Pop*. But there is one major and significant difference between the two. Mister *Iggy Pop* has worked hard on rocking and drugging his way to a fat free, sinewy anatomy enhanced by clearly visible veins and strange knots, while the similarly venous Savoy cabbage has done little more than lounging out in a vegetable field, basking in the sun, drinking water.

Which one of the two would you rather put in your own body? That is a matter entirely up to the opportunities that arise in life, the overall ambiance and your personal taste.

Savoy cabbage rolls *with lamb and chanterelles*

Preheat the oven to 345°F (175°C/Gas Mark 4). Grate the onion and apples on the coarse side of a shredder. Crush or chop the walnuts before toasting them lightly in a dry frying pan. Mix together onions, apple and nuts with ground lamb, crumbled cube of vegetable stock and cinnamon. Pepper generously.

Pour enough water in a large pot to cover about 4 inches (10cm) from the bottom and bring to a boil. Discard outer leaves of Savoy cabbage heads before peeling the remaining leaves off one by one, except the smallest at the core. Immerse a few leaves at a time into the boiling water for about a minute, then pick them up with the help of a perforated

1 large onion
2 apples
3½oz (100g) walnuts
13oz (400g) ground lamb
1 cube vegetable stock
½ teaspoon cinnamon
2 small heads of Savoy cabbage
7oz (200g) chanterelles
7fl oz (200ml) double cream
3 tablespoons whey cheese
2 tablespoons veal stock
10½fl oz (300ml) water

ladle and let cool. To make sure the cabbage leaves will be supple and easy to fold, cut off a wedge of the toughest part of the leaf rib. Grab a small amount of meat mixture and place on a cabbage leaf, then fold into a pretty parcel. Pack tightly in ovenproof dish.

Brush the chanterelles clean and chop them coarsely, fry in butter, add cream and whey cheese. Let the cheese dissolve before adding veal stock and water and bringing to a boil. Pour the chantarelle sauce over the cabbage rolls. Let cook in oven for about 40 minutes.

Serve with lingonberries and boiled potatoes.

Promise you'll never do what I tell you to

This is a book in which there are recipes. Every recipe contains a list of ingredients as well as more or less elaborate instructions on how to handle, divide, prepare, cook, add them and in what order.

All of this appears to be very precise and well thought out. And since it is written in (and printed) in a book, the reader may very well imagine that he or she is dealing with *The Big Fat Truth*.

However, that is not the case. You see, the author will not eat the food you cook from this book, but you will.

Recipes are tricky in nature. The two lemons stated in the list of ingredients may turn out to be one lemon too many if you happen to have come home with two unusually large or unusually sour fruits.

Exactly how much four cloves of garlic is varies from bulb to bulb. The heat in a fresh chilli varies; some have a sting that is only slightly less wimpy than that of the common red pepper (capsicum), others are so malicious that even half the suggested amount is enough to kill the entire dish and severely wound the people eating it.

And it gets worse. If your oven is a few years old or simply of a wilful nature, it may keep a considerably lower or higher temperature than the one you try to achieve with the help of the dial. Furthermore, the exact amount of salt or pepper that should go into the dishes you cook is a matter grown up people must decide on for themselves.

To cook food according to a recipe without tasting along the way is a bit like marrying a person someone else has picked out for you. *Don't do it.* In the middle of your face, you have a complete set of wonderful cooking tools. They're not intended merely for decorative purposes in the area between your hair and your chin, but they are there for you to use.

Look, *smell* and *taste* whatever is puttering in your pots. How does it taste, really? Happy that way? Or do you need to add any of the following?

Salt
Your first aid when the food tastes a little weak, flat and bland. Makes sleepy taste buds wake up with a jolt. Sharpens and intensifies flavour and contrast in other ingredients. It downplays raw, earthy flavours. *Add in the shape of:* Salt or one of the suggestions listed under *UMAMI*. *Tip:* Go light rather than heavy on the salt, as it's more tricky to correct the latter. And don't waste your expensive flake salt on paste water or your stew—neither you nor anyone else will notice the difference.

Pepper
Endows childish flavour with a more mature character, with a more distinct character. Brings and ties together the flavours of various ingredients, bestowing the food with a fiery elegance and bite. *Add in the shape of:* Freshly ground pepper from a pepper. Tip: Buy whole pepper corns of the most expensive kind you can find, give your dish an extra round of pepper about three minutes prior to serving and discover how much this spice rack stable can do for you and your food.

Acidity
Balances fat and salt, and makes flavours perkier, more alive and distinct. Furthermore possesses the enviable ability to startle the saliva glands, making your mouth water, literally. *Add in the shape of:* Lemon, lime, wine or vinegar, just to give a few examples.

Fat
Rounds off and takes the edge off harsh, metallic and other challenging flavours. Makes everything taste juicier, creamier, smoother and more pleasing. *Add in the shape of:* Cream, butter, coconut milk, cheese, oils, roasted nuts and seeds.

Sweetness
Beautifies, enhances and completes all other flavours. Complements and evens out sour and bitter elements. *Add in the shape of:* Sugar, honey, syrup, port, ketchup, balsamic vinegar, chutney.

Umami
Makes the food heartier by supplying the metallic quality that's a characteristic trait in foods such as aged cheese, air-dried ham, tasty broth and miso. *Add in the shape of:* Asian fish sauce, soy sauce, celery salt, tomato puree, anchovy, stock cube or stock concentrate.

Chinese pork *with calvados and ginger* **83**

On every pig, there are two fillets of pork, a rather dull variety of meat crowding the meat counters. On every pig there are also four shanks (two hands and two knuckles), cheap and tasty cuts you can only purchase by way of exception in your average grocery store. Considering how *few* shanks there are for sale compared to the insane amount of pork fillets people tuck in, there should be a huge mountain of shanks somewhere. I'm posing the question here: *Where is it?*

Where could you possibly hide loads of pink flesh so that no one can find it? How do you conceal a considerable amount of meat without making other people suspicious? What are the secrets, tricks, and methods? Keeping one's weight is not easy with this appetite.

We, the people, deserve to know the truth.

Chinese pork *with calvados and ginger*

Preheat the oven to 290°F (140°C/Gas Mark 2). Place the ham hocks in a large cast-iron pot, cover with lid and place in the oven for about 2½ hours. Remove from oven, let chill, trim away fat and rind and discard. Pick off the lean, tender meat from the bones and set aside.

Chop the onions finely and the garlic even finer and fry in olive oil over low heat for about 15 minutes or until the onions darken in colour and take on a sweet flavour.

Add whole tomatoes, water, cinnamon sticks, whole star anise, ground piri-piri, calvados, soy sauce, honey and the meat. Let simmer for about 30 minutes. Add rinsed beans, ginger juice (shred the ginger finely, then squeeze out the juice and discard the dry ginger fibre ball that remains) and generous amounts of freshly ground Szechwan pepper (you probably won't need to add salt, the meat is salty enough in itself).

2½ ham hocks, brined
3 onions
6 garlic cloves
1 can whole tomatoes
  + can of water
2 cinnamon sticks
6 whole star anise
2 piri-piri, dried
1¾fl oz (50ml)
  calvados
1 teaspoon Chinese
  soy sauce
1 tablespoon honey
1 can black beans or
  equivalent amount
  home-cooked
2 thumb-sized knobs
  of ginger
Szechwan pepper
  (or black pepper)
10 red plums

Cut the plums in wedges and add right before serving. Serve with cooked rice or thick udon noodles.

We've all heard of women, who, after having had their hearts broken, head for their terrible exes' apartments to cut big holes in their trousers. But when I was let down by love for the first time, I went to my terrible boyfriend's apartment, where I, foaming with rage, ate all his crispbread.

I ran into him a few years later. By then, he'd lost all his hair. I assume it was the shock that did it.

Baked trout *with butter fried lemon*

Preheat the oven to 500°F (250°C/Gas Mark 9). Pat the fish dry inside and out with kitchen paper, then rub with salt. Slice two of the lemons thinly and use to stuff the fish. Place in an ovenproof dish or roasting pan.

Cook in oven for 10 minutes or until the back fin comes off easily. Halve the remaining lemons and sprinkle a pinch of sugar over the

3–4 rainbow trout or
  arctic char, whole
  but gutted
4 lemons
1 teaspoon sugar
1¾oz (50g) butter
flatbread

cut side. Melt the butter in a frying pan. When the butter has ceased to bubble, put the lemons in the pan, cut-side down. Keep frying until the lemons take on some beautiful colour.

Serve the fish with boiled new potatoes, flake salt, the butter from the pan, butter fried lemons and flatbread.

In my childhood, the pumpkin was known primarily as a means of transportation. We heard about people in fancy clothes who rode inside pumpkins, going to fancy balls in fancy palaces. These days, pumpkins are available from the month of August in regular grocery stores. My personal favourite among the more common kinds is the *butternut squash*, a somewhat smaller variety with a pale yellow exterior, firm flesh and a sweet, buttery taste that's a wonderful contrast to the salty flavour of feta cheese and pork.

The most difficult thing about cooking with pumpkins is cutting it when it's still raw—the slippery peel and firm content makes it dangerously easy to slip with the knife, accidentally cutting of one's arms and legs. The best and safest way is to use a sword. Take a stride away from the pumpkin, wield the sword way over your head and cut all the way down through the pumpkin. If possible, wear armour.

Butternut squash *with feta cheese, pine nuts and lentils*

Preheat the oven to 340°F (175°C/Gas Mark 4). Halve, de-seed and cut the squash in 8 pieces, brush them with olive oil and place them in an ovenproof dish. Crumble feta cheese over the squash, sprinkle with pine nuts and drizzle with maple syrup. Cook in oven for about 40 minutes.

In a pot, bring plenty of water to a boil, pour the lentils in, remove from the heat and cover with lid. Let sit and swell for about 30 minutes before you bring the pot back to the stove and let the lentils simmer over very low heat for 10–15 minutes.

1 butternut squash
  (about 16oz/500g)
8oz (250g) feta
  cheese
2½oz (75g) pine nuts
1 tablespoon maple
  syrup
7oz (200g) green
  lentils, dried
2 packets of bacon
a few sage leaves
  (not necessary,
  but nice)

Dice the bacon and fry it crispy. Add finely chopped sage and drained lentils. Serve with the butternut squash.

Because our parents did not buy a colour TV until *1987*, my sisters and I spent many years of our childhood seeking audiovisual entertainment in other places. On Friday nights we'd often gather at our local grocery store to watch grilled chickens. Behind a yellow-tinged, grease-stained glass window, chicken rotated on their spits, *row after row* until their skins sparkled and glowed thanks to chicken grease and barbecue seasoning.

It was a spectacle more beautiful than the setting sun, even cosier than sitting by a crackling fire.

And fact remains that watching a roasting chicken still beats most of TV's repertoire. Especially if you'd consider zapping away from that constant re-run called the potato salad.

Corn fed chicken *with lavender and lemon*

Preheat the oven to 390°F (200°C/Gas Mark 6). Tear off the lavender leaves and chop finely —you'll only need about a tablespoon. Wash the lemon and grate the zest with a light and gentle hand (just the yellow part, no pith). Combine lavender and lemon zest with butter (at room temperature) and roughly a teaspoon of freshly squeezed lemon juice and stir into a smooth mixture. Detach the skin from breast and thighs, gently, so that the skin doesn't break.

Now, get in under the skin and stuff with lavender butter as best as you can. Be particularly generous at the breast section. Finish up by rubbing the entire exterior of the bird with fine salt.

3 sprigs of lavender
1 lemon
1¾oz (50g) butter, at room temperature
1 corn-fed chicken (about 3lb/1½kg)
1 slice white bread

Chop the remaining lavender coarsely, dice the lemon, mix with crumbled bread and stuff the bird as tightly as you can.

You'd do well to tie the bird's legs together. This way, the chicken keeps the stuffing better in place and cooks more evenly. Put in an ovenproof dish, breast facing up, and cook for 1 hour and 40 minutes. When only 10 minutes remain of the cooking time, turn the knob to grill for crispier skin.

Serve with a salad, sour cream and steamed summer vegetables.

Tip: For God's sake, don't eat the stuffing.

The *chevre chaud* was invented in 1914 by Frenchman Jean-Pierre Claudeville (1878–1942). It was an immediate hit and Claudeville spent the rest of his days touring the country with his sandwich grill and a backpack filled with goat's cheese.

On his deathbed, monsieur Claudeville confessed that he would rather have become a locomotive driver or an employment officer—and that to his mind, a thick slab of hot goat's cheese was not much of a dinner. Perhaps it would do, but only if you'd had enjoyed a hearty lunch earlier in the day.

I couldn't agree more. Chevre chaud is not much of a dinner; it is really much better suited as a dessert or as an appetiser.

Pears chevre chaud *with anise and almonds*

Preheat the oven to 440°F (225°C/Gas Mark 7), grill setting.

Roast the almonds in a dry frying pan until they begin to take on some colour.

Roast the anise seeds the same way, till they start smelling of liquorice. Crush the roasted anise seeds in a mortar and blend with honey and a generous pinch of flake salt. Halve, de-seed and slice the pears and

1¾oz (50g) almonds
½ teaspoon anise seeds
1¾fl oz (50ml) runny honey
pinch of flake salt
4 perfectly ripe pears
5oz (150g) soft goat's cheese

place the slices in an ovenproof dish (grease the dish with a little oil). Cut the goat's cheese in thin slices, put the cheese on top of the pears, the almonds on top of the cheese and drizzle honey over it all.

Gratinate the whole shebang on the top rack of your oven for about 5 minutes or until the cheese bubbles up and gets a little burned at the tips. Serve with port.

Pears chevre chaud *with anise and almonds* 93

Suddenly, you're not feeling well. You're not seriously ill, but there is something frail, weak and sullen about you. A quick look in the mirror confirms your suspicions; you're not looking all that great either, lacklustre and grey like an old potato. Now you're getting a little anxious. You google "weak, sullen and potato" but you don't seem to find any matching illness.

Perhaps there's a virus, you think to yourself, or is there a problem with the glands? Could it be that you're in the early stages of a serious deficiency disease despite a severe effort to eat spinach and cabbage at least three times a year? What are you missing? What vital substance are you lacking? *What is it that your body is trying to tell you?* And then, suddenly, you connect the dots and relief spreads through your body like hot chocolate sauce. The only trouble with you is this—you've had too little ice cream lately.

Peppermint ice cream *with chocolate sauce*

Bring out three large bowls. In the first, whisk egg yolks and icing sugar until light and fluffy. In the second bowl, beat egg whites and sugar into a stiff foam. In the third bowl, whip the cream. Carefully fold the yolk mixture into the whipped cream, and add the peppermint oil or food colouring. Just as gently, fold egg whites into the mixture. Pour into a mould, cover with cling film and put in freezer for at least 4 hours.

To make the chocolate sauce: combine golden syrup and sugar and bring to a boil while stirring until all sugar is dissolved. Add cocoa powder while whisking, then cream and salt. Let bubble over lowest possible heat (careful, don't let it burn) until it becomes thick and slightly sticky.

Bring the ice cream out of the freezer a bit before serving to let it thaw slightly, then serve with hot chocolate sauce.

Serves 8

Ice cream:
4 egg yolks
3½oz (100g) icing
 sugar
4 egg whites
4 tablespoons sugar
10fl oz (300ml)
 double cream
4 drops peppermint
 oil

Chocolate sauce:
1¾fl oz (50ml)
 golden syrup
1¾oz (50g) sugar
3½oz (100g) cocoa
 powder
2¾fl oz (100ml)
 double cream
pinch of salt

I was thinking of our child's birthday party. How about renting a party boat that we'll redecorate as a pirate's ship? You know, with face painting, dance machines and children's yoga on the lower deck, horseback riding and fireworks in the fore, keelhauling and laser dome on the upper deck, and live entertainment in the ballroom? I thought we could check with *Radiohead* or *The Jonas Brothers*.

I was also thinking we could hire Roald Dahl, have him come in and read from one of his books. Oh, he's dead? Bummer. Well then, let's settle for Colin Firth, he was great in *Nanny McPhee*. Let's keep this *a small affair*. Just the children at day care. Noah, Ellis, Freya, Alasdair, Otis, Miya, Uma, Ossy, Chloé, Buster, Luna, Myrrh, Bilbo, Embla, Britny, Ditten, Drutten, Ashley, Wilson, Jackson, Junior, Yolande, Gaston, Ezra, Beppo, Buppy, Legolas, Laban, Wolf, Alaska, Caesar, Moltas and Olsen's youngest, what's her name? Chaka Khan? Party favours, balloons, candy and dinner with place cards. But dear, the cake—what should we do about the cake?

Ice cream cake *extra deluxe*

If you want to make it easy on yourself, use three springform tins. And if you want to show off with perfect ice cream layers, line the rims of the tins with sturdy transparency paper, the type that people used for overhead presentations before there were laptops!

The ice cream layers:
Combine kinds of ice cream and divide between two springform tins. Be firm and push it around so it's evenly distributed. Put in freezer. Use a knife to cut the ice cream out when it's time to assemble the cake.

Assembling the cake:
Preheat the oven to 400°F (200°C/Gas Mark 6). Break up the chocolate into pieces and put in a bowl with the butter (cut in chunks). Bring out a pot, bring water to a boil, then place the bowl with chocolate and butter over it.

Remove from the heat once the chocolate has melted. Add the sugar and salt to the

210fl oz (6 litres)
  of ice cream,
  different kinds
7oz (200g) dark
  chocolate (at least
  72 per cent cocoa)
5oz (150g) butter
3½oz (100g)
  + 1 teaspoon sugar
pinch of salt
1¾oz (50g) plain flour
4 egg yolks
4 eggs
1 teaspoon cocoa
  powder
1 tub chocolate sauce
  or one batch home
  made, *see page 94*
fruit, berries, flowers
  and meringues for
  decoration

chocolate while stirring. Sift the flour into the batter and stir until smooth. Now, gently fold beaten egg yolks and eggs into the batter.

Grease the third springform tin. Mix a teaspoon each of sugar and cocoa powder and use to coat the tin. Pour the batter into the tin and bake for exactly 10 minutes. Remove from oven, let cool and then put in freezer for at least 2 hours—the cake is only half-baked and needs a little help in setting.

Liberate the cake from the tin with the help of a knife. Let it defrost a little bit before you assemble your masterpiece.

Assembling the cake:
Sit one ice cream layer on a large plate, pour a little chocolate sauce over it, place the chocolate cake on top, pour some more sauce over this layer then add the final ice cream layer on top. Decorate as beautifully as you can and serve immediately.

The *Jerusalem artichoke* is an unattractive, difficult to peel and surprisingly expensive root vegetable. The taste is delicious which, when you consider the high price, could fool you into thinking that it would be a great idea to grow your own. But beware! Beneath the humble exterior lurks a deceptive character, ready to change your life as you know it.

You see, the Jerusalem artichoke is related to the sunflower and it is very easy to grow. Simply put a few knobs into the ground and they'll take care of the rest. Soon you'll have tough, sturdy, man-high stalks all over your garden; in the front, in the back, in your favourite little sunny spot and further away—all over your neighbours' lawn. It won't be long before the artichokes seal off your only, tiny glimpse of the sea, block your garage door and enclose the entire house in a permanent, suffocating embrace. *My advice:* Buy organic artichokes and turn them into soup, *immediately*.

Jerusalem artichoke soup *with walnut croutons*

Peel and chop the onion, trim and dice the Jerusalem artichokes and potatoes. Fry the vegetables in olive oil for a little bit. Add water and stock. Let cook until the artichokes are nice and soft. Mix smooth in blender, add the cream and pour into pot. Bring to a boil. Season with salt and freshly ground pepper.

Dice the bacon and fry until crispy, then set bacon aside to drain on kitchen paper. Cut the edges off the bread and discard then cut the bread into squares. Fry in butter until golden. Mix with crumbled bacon and serve with the soup.

1 large onion
20oz (600g) Jerusalem
   artichokes
2 large potatoes
31fl oz (900ml) water
4 tablespoons veal
   stock concentrate
7fl oz (200ml) double
   cream
1 package of bacon
   rashers
4 slices of walnut
   bread
butter

Black eye

Butter bean

Kidney

Soba *with chicken and horseradish*

Soak the dried mushrooms overnight (save some of the soaking water for the stock if you like). Cook the noodles in plenty of salted water for 4 minutes or until they're almost done (the cooking time varies from brand to brand—so you have to try it for yourself). Drain and rinse the noodles in lukewarm water.

Pick the meat off the chicken and rip it into smaller pieces. Slice the mushrooms. Bring the stock to a boil and add soy sauce, sugar, vinegar, chicken meat and mushrooms. Taste and season with mushroom water, salt and pepper. Keep simmering.

Chop the scallions finely, cut the broccoli into florets. Add scallions, broccoli, rinsed beans and noodles to the stock, cover with lid and let cook for close to a minute. Ladle into bowls and serve with grated horseradish.

8 dried Chinese mushrooms (found in Asian grocery stores)
7oz (200g) soba noodles
½ grilled chicken
1 litre chicken stock (or 2 stock cubes or 2 tablespoons stock concentrate + water)
½ tablespoon dark Chinese soy sauce
1 tablespoon sugar
1 tablespoon rice vinegar
1 bundle scallions
1 bunch broccoli
1 can black beans or equivalent amount home-cooked
fresh horseradish

Where do you find the boldest food creatures in the world? I'd put my money on pizza bakers, a bunch of people who stretch boundaries and try out new, adventurous and often very strange combinations of ingredients, flavours and influences. *Döner meat*, *tenderloin* and *hot sauce* between generous layers of melted cheese? Yes please! *Pineapple*, *ham*, *banana* and *curry sauce* on a bread crust? Why not? Ground meat, taco sauce or sushi? The list goes on and on.

One of the main threats to great cooking is the fear of failing; an unwillingness to take risks, to just throw a few things together and hope for the best. To visit a pizza place, read the menu and take a moment to study the creations of free minds can be considered no less than therapy for more cowardly souls.

Pizza *with salami and grilled vegetables*

Preheat the oven to 400°F (200°C/Gas Mark 6). Slice onion and aubergine (eggplant) thinly, brush with olive oil and place on baking sheet lined with baking paper. Add halved cherry tomatoes, cut sides up. Roast in oven for about 30 minutes, open the oven door every now and then to let steam out.

Remove the vegetables and crank the heat up to maximum grill. If you own a pizza stone, this is the time to put it on a rack in the upper part of the oven—if you don't have a pizza stone, place an empty baking sheet there and let it warm up. Make the tomato sauce. Slice the artichoke hearts thinly and the mushrooms even more thinly. Shred the mozzarella, using the coarse side of a box grater.

Cover the pita breads with a very thin coating of tomato sauce. Add the shredded

To make 8 (rather small) pizzas:
4 onions
2 small aubergines (eggplants)
8oz (250g) cherry tomatoes
½ batch tomato sauce *(see page 28)*
2 cans artichoke hearts
20 fresh mushrooms
5 balls of mozzarella
8 large flat pita breads
24 thin slices of salami
yellow peperoncino
black olives (with pits) (save the olives and peperoncino for serving)

mozzarella, salami, mushrooms, artichoke hearts and grilled vegetables.

Now it's finally time for the pizzas to go into the oven. If you don't own a baking shovel (some people actually do), use a thin and light cutting board to transfer the pizzas to the pizza stone/baking sheet. Bake each pizza for 4–5 minutes and serve immediately.

Note: Yes, making your own pizza is a bit of a hassle but leftover pizza can be frozen and spread joy in the future!

Sauerkraut *(see page 11)* is surprisingly delicious with pizza.

Could his name have been Torbjörn? Short and stout with dainty little hands and a surprisingly snappy gait. I don't quite know who he was or who really knew him, but as time went on, he made a habit of coming to visit to give me various treats he loved for me to eat. Gooseberries. Cookies. Cheese. Fruit.

One day, he stopped by with a bottle of ale, a dried cod and a hammer, all of which he handed to me with his face beaming with expectation.

I was to pound off chips of the cod with the help of the hammer and wash it all down with the ale. The cod was tough and grey and dry as paper. It doesn't sound all that delicious to me, I said. *Oh, I thought you would understand*, Torbjörn sadly replied. I never saw him again.

Fish soup *with lentils and langoustines*

Soak the lentils for an hour. Chop the onions finely and the garlic even finer. Peel and finely dice the celeriac. Sweat onions, garlic and celeriac in a pot over medium heat. De-seed and finely chop the chilli. Add chilli, cumin, paprika and saffron and cook for a minute. Add passata or chopped tomatoes, water and drained lentils. Let simmer for about 15 minutes or until the lentils are cooked but not mushy (go ahead, taste them). Add stock cubes.

Wash the lemon and zest the peel (be light on your hand), then juice the lemon. Add all the zest to the soup and season with lemon juice, salt and freshly ground pepper. Cut the fish in pieces and add. Let simmer for two minutes, push langoustines halfway down into the soup and serve.

5oz (150g) beluga
   lentils, dried
2 onions
4 cloves of garlic
¼ celeriac
1 red chilli
½ teaspoon cumin,
   ground
2 teaspoons paprika
½g saffron
1 can or tetra sieved
   passata or chopped
   tomatoes
35fl oz (1 litre) water
3 chicken stock cubes
1 lemon
13oz (400g) fish fillet
4 langoustines

Every now and then, the thought of making one's own sushi arises. How hard can it be, you think. Isn't it all about simply silencing the inner critic and *just go for it*? The ability to cook food is, after all, innate, just waiting to be put to work. The everyday movements like the repetitive rhythm of the knife slicing food on a cutting board or the swirling motion of a ladle stirring a pot has been etched into humanity through thousands of generations. First, a child learns to crawl, then stand and shortly thereafter it's mature enough to go fetch a pot and whip up a bechamel. Or to churn butter. Or roll sushi.

So what is it exactly you're waiting for, you ask yourself. And then it hits you: You're waiting for dinner to be ready already. Preferably today. And that's where I come in, suggesting something that tastes suspiciously like sushi, but that is ready in 15 minutes.

Sugar fried salmon *with noodles*

Skin the salmon. Mix flake salt with the two tablespoons of sugar and pat the mixture onto both sides of the fish. Set aside.

Halve the cucumber, then shred it finely lengthwise, using a potato peeler. Halve the avocados, remove and discard the pit then spoon out and slice the green flesh. Roast the sesame seeds in a dry frying pan until they begin to take on a tiny bit of colour. Remove from heat and set aside.

Combine rice vinegar with sugar and stir until the sugar has dissolved completely.

In a large pot, bring a generous amount of water to a boil. Once it's boiling, heat some oil in a frying pan. Drop the noodles into the boiling water just as you put the

13oz (400g) fresh
  salmon fillet
1 tablespoon flake salt
2 tablespoons sugar
½ cucumber
2 avocados
2 tablespoons sesame
  seeds
1¾fl oz (50ml) rice
  vinegar
1¾oz (50g) sugar
1 packet (8oz/250g)
  rice noodles
gari
wasabi
japanese soy sauce

salmon in the pan—they will be ready at the same time! Be careful, salmon burns easily.

Sprinkle sesame seeds over the fried salmon, dress the drained noodles with the sweetened rice vinegar and serve with cucumber, avocado, gari, wasabi and Japanese soy sauce.

Melon salad
with cucumber and coriander

Halve, de-seed and cut the melon in slices, trim off rind and cut the fruit flesh in chunks. Shred the cucumber very, very finely, using a potato peeler or a Mandolin shredder. Peel and chop the red onion very, very finely. Chop the coriander, the whole plant, stems and all (if you choose mint the leaves are enough).

Squeeze the limes. Whisk together the lime juice and sugar, taste and season with salt and Tabasco. Combine fruit and dressing and serve.

1 galia melon,
   perfectly ripe
1 cucumber,
   preferably organic
½ red onion
1 pot fresh coriander
   or mint
2 limes
1 tablespoon sugar
green Tabasco (amount
   according to your taste)

Melon salad *with cucumber and coriander* **115**

Where should you look for inspiration for new, adventurous cooking? There are many different approaches. Some people prefer to travel to faraway lands to experience new cuisines, while others are content by simply opening the doors to their kitchen cupboards.

Isn't that a food processor hiding in there, way in, huddled up in the corner, surrounded by crumbs? It certainly is. It's been a while. Then again, you've never been big on cleaning out the cupboards. The food processor. How about mixing something? Like a smooth creamy soup and…minced fish?

And voilà, you're just as inspired as those who go the distance to sit on a tropical beach with sand in their undies, slurping rum from a coconut.

Fish cakes *with warm avocado soup*

Soup:
Whip cream. Remove and discard the pits from avocados, then spoon out avocado meat. Using a food processor, mix avocado, de-seeded and finely sliced chilli, milk and lemon juice into a smooth puree. Stop the machine and carefully fold in whipped cream. Bring the stock to a boil. Add the avocado cream mixture and heat. Season with salt.

Fish cakes:
Defrost, peel and chop the shrimp coarsely. Put aside in a cool place. Cut the fish in small chunks and process with fish sauce, salt, egg white and coconut cream into a pliable mince.

De-seed and finely slice the chilli, peel and finely chop garlic and ginger. Fold into the fish mixture together with the shrimp. Rub a little oil between the palms of your hands and use them to shape little patties that you dip into breadcrumbs and fry in oil until they're golden on both sides. Serve with the soup.

Soup:
7fl oz (200ml) double
    cream
2 ripe avocados
1–2 green chillies
7fl oz (200ml) milk
½ lemon
14fl oz (400ml)
    chicken stock

Fish cakes:
16oz (500g) (cooked)
    shrimp with shells
10oz (300g) skinned
    and boned fish fillet
    (suitable varieties are
    hoki, pikeperch,
    perch or cod) may be
    bought frozen and
    used half-defrosted
1 tablespoon fish sauce
    + pinch of salt

1 egg white
5fl oz (150ml)
    coconut cream
1 red chilli
1 small garlic clove
1 small piece of fresh
    ginger
breadcrumbs,
    preferably Panko,
    a Japanese variety

People often say that they are *full to the gills*, meaning they've eaten a *whole lot*. But even a quick analysis of the expression will reveal that you're never really reaching the gills simply by putting food in your mouth. You see, the gills are not found *inside the throat*, but on *the outside*. If you're really looking to be full to the gills, you'd have to shovel food into your face with such speed and gusto that some food would trickle down your face all the way down your neck to finally gather in the gill area.

And that's all I have to say in this matter.

Chicken patties *with mango chutney and coconut rice*

If you have the time: Let the coconut flakes soak in a little milk for 20 minutes or more.

Using a food processor, chop the chicken thigh fillets to a moderately coarse mince. Roast the cardamom for a minute in a dry pan until it starts to give off aroma, then crush it in a mortar. Combine chicken mince, cardamom, egg, breadcrumbs, salt and (drained) coconut flakes.

Shape the chicken mixture into plump patties and fry golden on both sides in a little butter or oil. Cover with lid and let cook until done for another 10 minutes over low heat.

Coconut rice:
Combine rice, coconut milk, water and salt in a cooking pot. Press down the lime

1¾oz (50g) coconut flakes
16oz (500g) chicken thigh fillets
1 teaspoon cardamom, whole seeds
1 egg
1¾oz (50g) breadcrumbs
½ teaspoon salt
10oz (300g) uncooked basmati rice
1 can coconut milk
7fl oz (200ml) water
pinch of salt
4 lime leaves (if you like, can be skipped)

leaves. Cook as you'd usually cook rice, but on somewhat lower temperature, for close to 20 minutes or until the rice has absorbed all liquid.

Serve the chicken patties with coconut rice, mango chutney and lime wedges.

Chicken patties *with mango chutney and coconut rice* **119**

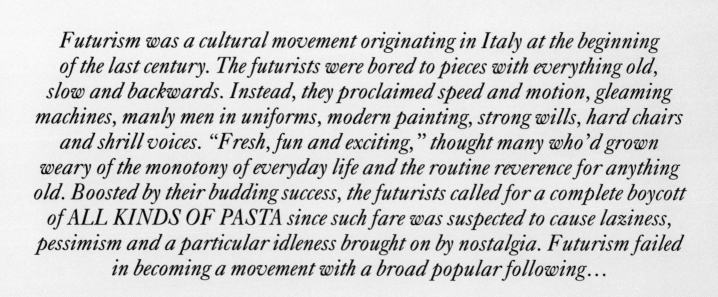

Futurism was a cultural movement originating in Italy at the beginning of the last century. The futurists were bored to pieces with everything old, slow and backwards. Instead, they proclaimed speed and motion, gleaming machines, manly men in uniforms, modern painting, strong wills, hard chairs and shrill voices. "Fresh, fun and exciting," thought many who'd grown weary of the monotony of everyday life and the routine reverence for anything old. Boosted by their budding success, the futurists called for a complete boycott of ALL KINDS OF PASTA since such fare was suspected to cause laziness, pessimism and a particular idleness brought on by nostalgia. Futurism failed in becoming a movement with a broad popular following…

Spaghetti *with pea pesto*

Bring plenty of salted water to a boil in a large pot, and some more water for the peas in a smaller pot. Bring out your food processor. Grate the Parmesan. Chop the mint leaves.

When the water is boiling in both pots, throw the pasta into the big pot and the peas into the smaller. Cook the peas for close to a minute, drain, then mix the hot peas with Parmesan, mint and cashew nuts to a smooth pesto together with the olive oil. Right before the spaghetti is done, scoop up half

3½oz (100g) Parmesan
1 pot fresh mint
16oz (500g) spaghetti
10oz (300g) green peas
3½oz (100g) cashew nuts, unsalted
1¾fl oz (50ml) olive oil
1 knob of butter
1 lemon

a small cup of the pasta water into which you let a piece of butter melt. Drain the cooked pasta in a colander, bring back into the pot, add the buttered water and stir. Serve the pasta with the pea pesto, lemon wedges and a revolutionary mind.

Tip: Asparagus wrapped in Parma ham, fried crispy in butter or olive oil is great with this *(see page 122)*. Actually, I can't think of a single thing this kind of asparagus isn't great with.

Oh, so you're not the kind of person who makes poached salmon? The method *is not really your cup of tea.* In fact, the thought of walking out to the kitchen to poach salmon is about as foreign to you as the concept of getting on a sailboat to sit there all by yourself until the boat has sailed all around the world.

Then how about this: *Perhaps that is the reason why you should poach some salmon.* Perhaps it's time to challenge your self-image and all the prejudice you have regarding the things you should and shouldn't do? You begin by poaching salmon and discover that you actually like it. Next thing you know is that you also enjoy wearing high hats, walking around naked, becoming a troubadour and sending conspiracy theories to your local newspaper.

This could be the beginning of something new, something exciting.

Poached salmon *with roasted potato salad*

Place a large ovenproof dish on top of a thick towel. Cut the salmon in 1-inch (2cm) thick slices and place in the dish. In a pot, combine water together with sliced lemon and onion, bay leaves, salt, sugar and pepper corns, and bring to a boil. Pour the hot water over the salmon, cover the dish and set aside until chilled. Remove the salmon from liquid in time for serving.

Preheat the oven to 400°F (200°C/Gas Mark 6). Scrub the potatoes and cook them until they are halfway done, about 7 minutes. Cut the potatoes in ½-inch (1cm) thick slices. Slice the garlic finely. Shred the artichoke bottoms on the coarse side of a box grater, then distribute the shredded artichoke evenly in a roasting pan. Place the sliced potatoes and garlic on top. Drizzle with oil but save about 1 tablespoon. Cook until done in the upper part of the oven—push the contents around every now and then and remove from oven once potatoes take on a golden brown colour.

Roast the almonds in a dry frying pan until they take on plenty of colour, then chop them coarsely. Wash the lemons and grate the zest with a light and gentle hand (just the

Poached salmon:
20oz (600g) (thick) salmon fillet
35fl oz (1 litre) water
1 lemon
1 onion
3 bay leaves
1 tablespoon salt
1¾oz (50g) sugar
5 whole pepper corns

Roasted potato salad:
32oz (1kg) new potatoes or almond potatoes
3 garlic cloves
1 can artichoke bottoms
2¾fl oz (100ml) olive oil
½ tablespoon flake salt
3½oz (100g) almonds
2 lemons
2 teaspoons runny honey
1 pot fresh Thai basil or regular fresh basil

yellow part, no pith). Squeeze the juice from one of the lemons. Whisk together zest, lemon juice, remaining olive oil and honey.

Place the roasted potatoes in a bowl; add almonds and dressing while the potatoes are still piping hot and sprinkle with chopped herbs right before serving.

Panna cotta is a northern Italian pudding type invention that consists primarily of heavy cream. The fact the panna cotta has also managed to become popular way up in the very north of Europe is nothing short of a mystery, as northern people have never been good at handling cream in a calm and collected way.

Nowhere else in the world do people regard the concept of cream with as intense feelings of passionate yearning and terrified fear. Nowhere else does cream represent such intense connotations of both indulgence and decay. Only in northern Europe is cream seen as the very personification of the highest possible quality and the lowest moral. What begins with a thimble of cream will no doubt end in Dickensian misery, cardiac arrest and, finally, death.

"Mama mia!" the Italian dessert chefs say, shaking their heads in disbelief at our exaggerated concerns. *"Exchange half of the heavy cream for milk if you're so afraid of the delicious fat."*

Almond panna cotta *with warm cherries*

Preheat oven to 500°F (250°C/Gas Mark 9) grill. Soak gelatine leaves in cold water for about 10 minutes. Reduce the Amaretto to about half its amount by cooking it in a small thick-bottomed saucepan (this will also take about 10 minutes). Add cream and sugar and bring to a boil. Remove from stove, drain the soaked gelatine leaves and whisk into cream mixture. Pour into small moulds, cocottes or glasses. Leave to set in fridge for at least 3 hours.

Pit the cherries (this bit can be done in advance) and put them, cut sides up, on a

Serves 6:
2½ gelatine leaves
1¾fl oz (50ml) almond
  liqueur, Amaretto
  DiSaronno
17fl oz (500ml)
  double cream
  (or use half cream
  and half milk)
2 tablespoons sugar
5oz (150g) cherries
2 tablespoons sugar

baking tray lined with baking paper. Sprinkle with sugar and place on top rack in oven and bake for close to 5 minutes. Serve the cherries warm with the panna cotta.

Almond panna cotta *with warm cherries* **127**

There are couples' dinners with people you know. And then there are *spontaneous couples' dinners* with people you don't know but just happened to invite for dinner cause you suddenly felt an urge to look at some new faces over the dinner table. After a month or so, you'll get an invitation to come for dinner at the house of this new couple and once you're about to go home you make plans to see each other again—and this continues until every weekend is booked with dinners with various couples until you never have time to see your old friends again.

In the end, you begin to wish that all those hungry couples could think of that very first dinner as a kind of one-night stand, something that *felt right at the time* but shouldn't have to be repeated over and over again.

That's when the time is ripe for a recipe that divides. That makes the guests a little uncomfortable, mumbling things along the lines of "We don't know how to top this" or "You've outdone yourself, we couldn't possibly cook at this level", making it hard for them to ever invite you back. That kind of cooking. Is this the recipe you need?

I'm afraid it isn't. This is the most foolproof, social recipe, the one that you once used for that first dinner, the very reason all those bores became so attracted to you in the first place.

Lamb shanks *with fruit and couscous*

Trim away as much visible fat as possible from the lamb shanks. Pour a little oil in a frying pan and fry the lamb shanks all over, remove from the heat and set aside.

Chop the shallots finely and sweat till translucent in oil in a large pot. Add the lamb shanks and pour over the entire bottle of wine and as much additional water as you need to cover the meat. Cover and let simmer for 1½ hours. Remove the lid and let simmer for 30 more minutes (skim fat off from the

4 lamb shanks
4–5 shallots
1 bottle of Chablis
   or Chardonnay
   (unwooded)
3½oz (100g) almonds
4 peaches/nectarines
   or 8 apricots
¾oz (25g) butter
7fl oz (200ml) couscous
1 pot fresh mint

surface). Taste and season the stew with salt and freshly ground pepper.

Meanwhile, blanch the almonds. Pit the peaches and cut them into wedges. Add almonds, fruit, butter and couscous to the stove. (Make sure the couscous is soaked in liquid.) Remove from heat and serve within 5 minutes.

Top each serving with finely chopped fresh mint.

The *Minestrone* is one of the cornerstones of Italian cooking. If you've ever wondered what the Roman infantry was fed after a long day's march, it was likely a piping hot pot of minestrone. Can you picture it? The sun is slowly setting on a sky that's darkening in the east. On a lush field, a large number of Italian men, wearing sandals, pleated skirts and fancy helmets are forming a queue to a man-sized soup kettle. There's a rattling sound, no doubt coming from all the swords and harnesses. All the men share the same desire —you can see the yearning for soup glowing in their red-rimmed eyes. They're all wondering what might be in the soup today. Celeriac? Cabbage? Diced enemy meat? You never quite know with a minestrone.

Then again, it's only *half* as secretive as the smooth, mixed soup that refuses to give you any information at all beyond colour and taste.

Pumpkin soup *with roasted garlic*

Preheat the oven to 200°F (200°C/Gas Mark 6). Put a whole squash, onion and garlic (with the skins still on) on a baking sheet in the middle of the oven. Roast the garlic for close to 20 minutes, the squash and onion for about 50 minutes. Remove from oven and let the onion and squash cool off a little.

Halve, de-seed and scoop out the squash with the help of a spoon. Make a small incision at the base of the onion and squeeze out the softened contents. Peel the garlic cloves. Wash the lemon and grate the zest with a light and gentle hand (just the yellow part, no pith).

1 butternut squash
  (about 3lb/1½kg)
1 large onion
4 garlic cloves
1 lemon
7fl oz (200ml) double
  cream
1 tablespoon honey
2 tablespoons
  chicken stock
  concentrate
21fl oz (600ml) water
Parmesan cheese

Mix squash, onion, garlic, lemon zest, cream and honey into a thick puree.

Bring chicken stock and water to a boil. Add the puree to the stock while stirring, taste and season with freshly squeezed lemon juice, salt and pepper. Heat and serve with grated Parmesan cheese (and crispy fried bacon for those who crave such things).

Why is lamb such a fatty meat? How is it possible? Do lambs treat themselves to double pastries for tea? Do they take the car to the grocery store to stock up on *chips* and *candy* every weekend? Do they skip breakfast, lunch and dinner to stagger up in the middle of the night, to head for the freezer to get out a whole pizza to eat, huddled over the kitchen sink? *No, no, a thousand times no.* The little lamb skips around in the meadow, eating only vegetarian fare. Slow carbs from, you know it, grass. And yet, the lamb keeps gaining weight. It must feel so unfair. Especially considering the fact that there are swine out there who can *gobble down any amount of food* without gaining a pound.

Lamb cassoulet *with sweet spices*

Cook the dried beans according to the express method described on page 9. Trim away as much fat as possible from the lamb, then fry the meat lightly in a little oil. Remove from heat and put aside.

In a large pot, fry finely chopped onion and garlic in olive oil. Pestle paprika, saffron, cloves, cumin and cardamom with sugar and salt in a mortar until you have a fine powder. Add the spice powder to the fried onions and let it all fry for a minute before you add tomatoes, cinnamon sticks, harissa, the lamb and as much water (or white wine) you need to cover the meat.

Using a potato peeler or a fruit knife, peel off the zest—the outermost orange part of the orange peel—in one long ribbon and place on top of everything else in the pot (to be fished out before serving). Cover with lid and let simmer for about 2 hours.

7oz (200g) large white beans (dried) or 2 cans ready cooked
5lb (2½kg) lamb shoulder, cut in big chunks
2 onions
4 garlic cloves
½ tablespoon paprika
1g saffron
3 cloves
1 tablespoon cumin
1 teaspoon cardamom, whole seeds
1 tablespoon sugar
1 teaspoon salt
1 can cherry tomatoes
2 cinnamon sticks
½ tablespoon harissa
1 orange, organic
4 (uncooked) merguez sausages

Taste and season with salt and pepper, add the cooked beans and the sausage, cut in pieces. Let simmer for another 5 minutes, remove the orange peel and serve.

Harvest time. Savour those two words! Wouldn't you agree they are words that simply beg you to put on your wooliest sweater and your longest skirt and walk about in nature until your cheeks are positively glowing? Stuff your pockets with berries and fruits, moss and old sticks you can arrange in a nice ceramic jug when you get home? Pass a bridge over troubled water. Make a nice fire and drink tea from a cup you hold onto with both your hands while you gaze into the distance. *Harvest time.* Old man searching for a heart of gold or a maid. Somewhere close to a lake.

Enough about harvest time, let's change the topic of conversation. And finish your almond cake. All of it. Every little crumble. Thank you.

Almond cake *with fruit and berries*

Preheat the oven to 340°F (175°C/Gas Mark 4).
Sift flour into a bowl. Add sugar, butter and egg and pinch into a dough. Set aside in cool place for an hour. Roll out dough and use to cover a regular pie mould or a few small ones.

Shred almond paste on the coarse side of a grater, then mix with sugar and butter. Add eggs, one at a time, and the egg yolk (save the lone egg white for the icing).

Stir into a smooth batter and pour into the pie crust. Cut fruit into pretty pieces (no need to cut the berries, though) and press into the batter. Bake on middle rack of oven for about 35 minutes or until cake is nice and golden. Set aside to cool.

Mix icing sugar with egg white to make icing. Drizzle icing over the cake. Enjoy.

Shortcrust:
13oz (400g) flour
3½oz (100g) sugar
4oz (125g) butter, at
    room temperature
1 egg

Filling:
10oz (300g) almond
    paste
2 tablespoons sugar
5oz (150g) butter, at
    room temperature
2 eggs
1 egg yolk
fruit and berries of
    your liking and

(perhaps) picking,
such as pears,
plums, cherries,
nectarines, apricots,
gooseberries,
currants,
blackberries

Icing:
5oz (150g) icing sugar
1 egg white

Almond cake *with fruit and berries* **137**

This recipe is a roaring, scornful laugh at sensible meals, the safety belt, the bicycle helmet, cholesterol alarms, food and nutrition recommendations and all those dreary people who insist on calling food "*diet*".

Because this is not a dish you'd associate with a diet, in any sense of the word. This is creamy sensualismus on a plate, a shameless, advanced seduction number, a dinner that will infallibly end with a couch full of guests with their trousers unbuttoned, huffing and puffing with their hands stroking their bulging tummies. *Dessert, anyone?* Wouldn't think so. If you'd wish for anything after this meal, it's more likely to be a round with a defibrillator. Then a cab, going home.

Lemon linguine *with trout roe and scallops*

Pour a generous amount of olive oil into a small bowl, salt and pepper the scallops, then add them to the oil and stir.

Whisk the egg yolks. Wash the lemons and grate the zest with a light and gentle hand (just the yellow part, no pith). Squeeze just one of the lemons. Grate the Parmesan finely. Whisk together egg yolks, lemon zest, lemon juice and cream until blended, then add the Parmesan. Set aside.

Boil water for the pasta in a large pot, salt generously and cook the pasta al dente.

olive oil
12 large scallops
4 egg yolks
2 lemons
3½oz (100g) Parmesan cheese
10oz (300ml) double cream
13oz (400g) linguine
¾oz (25g) butter
1¾oz (50g) trout roe

Meanwhile, fry the scallops, 1 minute on each side, in a very hot, teflon-coated frying pan. Drain the pasta using a colander, pour back into the pot, add the butter and then the lemon sauce. Heap up the pasta on the heated plates, top with scallops and trout roe. Serve immediately. I mean it.

Tip: This dish needs a little help in keeping warm. I suggest you heat the plates in your microwave oven or in the oven (15 minutes at 220°F/100°C/Gas Mark 1) prior to serving.

This is not really so much a recipe as it is two recipes: One is quick and easy and the result is delicious. The other is a little slower but also results in a delicious meal. The quick version is made from ready grilled, store bought chicken, the somewhat fussier version is made from fresh chicken—but the great thing is that no matter which one you pick, *you're a winner*.

The majority of the people giving this recipe a chance will take the road most travelled, going for store grilled chicken, happy and content about all the time and effort they've saved this way. Which in turn adds extra flavour to the soup for the very few who appreciate the sublime satisfaction that comes from being that remarkable person who cooks his or her ribollita *from scratch*, using only the finest, fresh ingredients.

Ribollita *with crispy fried chicken skin*

Chop the garlic finely. Peel and dice carrots and celeriac. Fry garlic, carrots and celeriac in a bit of oil in a large stockpot until the vegetables take on some colour. Add stock concentrate and fry some more. Pour over water and add bay leaves.

If you're cooking with store grilled chicken:
Strip the skin off the bird, chop it finely and put aside for later. Break the meat into bone-free chunks and add to the soup.

If you're cooking with fresh chicken:
Skin the uncooked chicken (this is a little easier if you begin by cutting the bird into four pieces), chop the skin finely and put aside for later.

Add the skinned chicken to the stock and let simmer till the chicken is cooked—this

2 garlic cloves
2 carrots
¼ celeriac
2 tablespoons chicken stock concentrate
35fl oz (1 litre) water
3 bay leaves
1 ready-grilled chicken or fresh chicken
7oz (200g) dry-cured streaky bacon
1 leek
1 small head Savoy cabbage
1 can small white beans or equivalent amount home cooked

will take roughly 30 minutes. Bring the chicken out of the soup and let cool. Break up the meat into bone-free chunks and return them to the soup.

From now on, everyone can join in, no matter which kind of chicken you're working with:
Dice and fry the bacon till crispy. Set aside. Now, add sliced leek and finely shredded Savoy cabbage (trim the cabbage from limp leaves, the tough base of the root and the most coarse veins, which tend to have a bitter taste). Add rinsed beans and let simmer for close to 10 minutes. Taste and season with salt and freshly ground black pepper. Meanwhile, fry the chopped chicken skin like you would fry bacon.

Top every bowl of soup with bacon and crispy fried chicken skin.

Every now and then, people wake up, stretch and yawn and hear themselves say, *"Know what? Today, I'm quitting my well-paid position at……to try my wings as a poet/fortune-teller/cookbook writer/cultural entrepreneur!"*

And then they…don't, with very few exceptions. But quite often, those exceptional people turn out to be very happy with their choices. They become poor, almost without exception. At their poorest, they borrow money from their parents and live on root vegetables and onions. It's rough, but manageable.

But it's much more manageable if you simply add two things: chicken and creme fraiche.

Chicken stew *with oven roasted root vegetables*

Preheat the oven to 400°F (200°C/Gas Mark 6). Peel and cut onions, parsnips, sweet potatoes and carrots into wedges and chunks. Place in roasting pan together with the garlic, broken up in cloves (but skins still intact). Drizzle with olive oil and roast in oven—the garlic for 20 minutes, the rest until the root vegetables have taken on a beautiful golden colour with a few brownish tips.

Use a garlic press to press the cloves (yes, with the skins still on). Wash the lemon and grate the zest with a light and gentle hand (just the yellow part, no pith), then squeeze the lemon. Whisk together pressed garlic, zest and lemon juice as well as finely chopped fresh thyme, a bit of olive oil and flake salt. Dress the root vegetables with the dressing right before serving.

Trim the chicken breasts and fry them a little, on the skin side only, until they've taken on a beautiful colour. Remove from the pan and cut the chicken in wide strips. Bring wine and chicken stock to a boil and add the chicken. Let simmer for about 5 more minutes. Thicken with creme fraiche and add finely chopped tarragon. Serve chicken stew with the oven roasted vegetables.

2 onions
2 parsnips
4 small sweet potatoes
2 carrots
½ garlic knob (or use 1 tablespoon garlic puree, *see page 10*)
1 lemon
½ pot fresh thyme
1 teaspoon flake salt
2–4 chicken breasts with skin
10fl oz (300ml) dry Riesling wine
17fl oz (500ml) chicken stock (water + 1 tablespoon chicken stock concentrate)
7fl oz (200ml) creme fraiche
1 pot fresh French tarragon

148 Chicken stew *with oven roasted root vegetables*

Are fruits female and vegetables male? If so, the avocado must be the least understood individual in the veggie section. Its very name means testicle in the ancient tongue of the Aztec people. We treat it like a vegetable. But it is in fact a *fruit*, a stone-fruit if you want to be even more specific.

Perhaps that's the reason why the avocado becomes so excited and cooperative when it, as in this dessert, is being served as the fruit it is. Just make sure you slice it thinly or it will steal the entire show.

Fruit carpaccio *with mango, citrus and avocado*

Combine vanilla powder or contents of the vanilla bean with creme fraiche and icing sugar. Season with freshly squeezed lemon juice. Using a pestle, grind sugar, star anise and cloves into a fine powder in a mortar.

Trim the oranges and grapefruit of peel, pith and membranes, then slice the flesh thinly. Peel mangoes using a potato peeler. Then slice the mango thinly, from the thick sides of the fruit all the way to the flat core.

Halve the avocados, discard the pit, carefully remove the flesh from the peel, then slice as thinly as you can, preferably on a Mandolin shredder. Arrange fruit on a large plate. Pour over juice from oranges and grapefruit. Sprinkle spiced sugar over the fruit and serve with creme fraiche.

1 pinch vanilla powder
(powdered vanilla
bean, found among
baking supplies)
or 1 vanilla bean
7 fl oz (200ml) creme
fraiche
2 tablespoons icing sugar
a few drops of lemon
juice
2 tablespoons sugar
1 star anise
2 cloves
3 oranges
1 pink grapefruit
2 mangoes
2 avocados

Chorizo skewers *with vegetables and figs*

If using wooden skewers (you need 8 for this recipe)—let them soak in water for a few hours prior to grilling. That way they don't catch fire as easily. Heat up the barbecue. Wait for the embers to get just perfect.

Cut the halloumi into 8 pieces. Halve the figs and wrap them in ham.

Cut away and discard the tough parts of the fennel like the side shoots. Cut the fennel into chunks (I know it's tricky to make them stick together, so let the skewers do their magic).

Cut the peppers (capsicums) in wedges. Thread chorizo, vegetables, halloumi and figs onto the skewers and, if you like, brush them with a little oil. Push the embers towards the middle of the grill, place the skewers along the sides of the grill rack, bring the lid down (if there is a lid) and grill a few minutes on each side.

7oz (200g) halloumi cheese
4 fresh figs
8 slices Parma or Serrano ham
1 fennel bulb
2 bell peppers (capsicums)
8 small chorizos or 4 large ones

Squid skewers *with salmon and lime*

Again, this will make 8 skewers. Cut each squid tube into four pieces and then each piece into two. Cut the salmon into four individual fillets and then cut each fillet into four smaller pieces.

Halve the limes and trim away the white core. Thread squid and salmon onto the skewers with lime leaves in between the fish. Top each skewer with a lime half.

Grill as for the chorizo skewers.

2 squid tubes
13oz (400g) salmon fillet
4 limes
32 lime leaves

Fruit skewers *with orange blossom syrup*

Whisk together orange blossom water, the juice from the lemons, sugar and water in a thick-bottomed pot over medium heat until sugar has dissolved completely.

Keep bubbling over lowest possible heat until the mixture has reduced to about half its original content. Whisk vanilla powder into the mixture and set aside to cool off.

Peel the pineapple and cut the flesh into chunks. Let the mangoes keep their skin and cut them where they are widest, as close to the flat core as possible. Cut each piece in two. Trim away the tough ends of the kiwis and halve the remaining fruit. Peel and cut the bananas into chunks.

Thread fruit onto skewers and grill as for the other skewers on this page, but make sure the grill rack is clean! Drizzle orange blossom syrup over the skewers and serve.

2¾fl oz (100ml) orange blossom water (found in Asian grocery stores)
2 lemons
3½oz (100g) sugar
1¾fl oz (50ml) water
pinch vanilla powder (powdered vanilla bean, found among baking supplies)

For 8–12 skewers:
1 pineapple
2 mangoes
4 kiwis
2 bananas
or other fruit of choice

The recipes are calculated to yield roughly 8 skewers each (you may get more or less, depending on how big you cut the chunks and how much you think is decent for each skewer); 3–4 skewers per person is about right. Serve with baked potatoes or coconut rice, *page 118*, and a salad like the one on *page 68*.

Chorizo skewers *with vegetables and figs.* Squid skewers *with salmon and lime.* Fruit skewers *with orange blossom syrup* 153

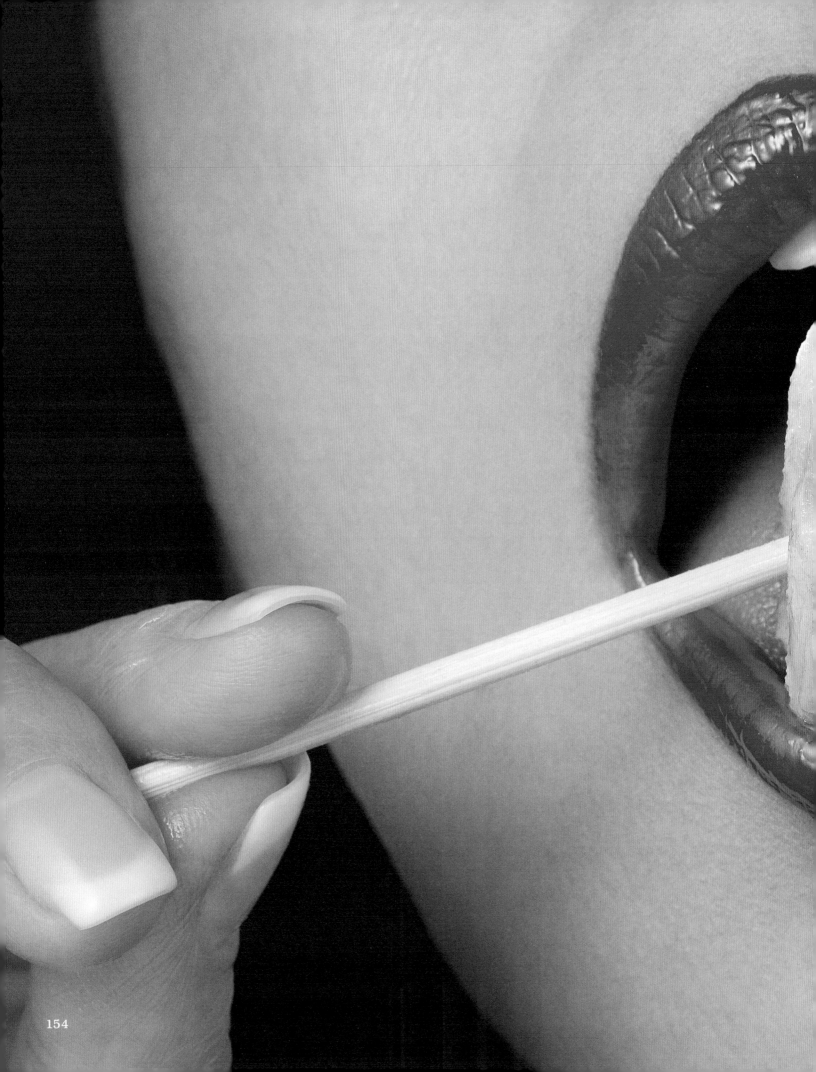

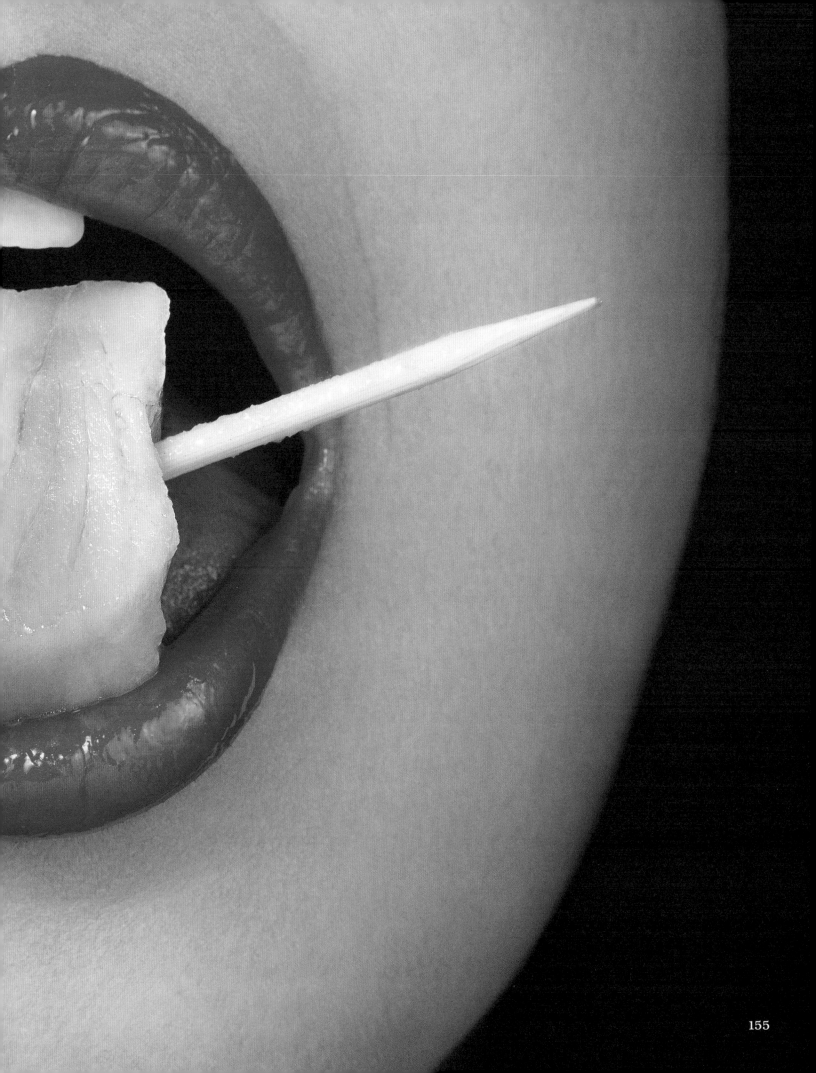

One of the world's most worthless creatures has to be the cavefish, an animal that spends his life standing behind a big rock, jaws wide open, pale-eyed and miserably unappealing while waiting for the moment when a somewhat smaller animal will swim into its mouth. Partly, this behaviour could be explained by survival tactics, but the alert observer also notices something else here—an unusually gloomy attitude towards life in general: *never contribute, if it works it works, just give me my little fish already*.

The cavefish lives at great depths so the chance that you'll run into one is very small. But the risk of running into its human equivalent is all the greater—the person who's always busy when it's time for you to move, who's forgotten his wallet again, who will shamelessly claim your stuff once you decide to part ways and who will, to the end of his days, fight for his rights to eat well but who will just as fiercely refuse to learn how to cook.

Did that last sentence hit a nerve? Good. Pull yourself together and cook this tonight.

Crispy minced salmon *with toasted rice*

Heat the cooking oil in a frying pan. Once hot, add the uncooked rice and gently tilt the pan from side to side to make sure the rice is evenly distributed.

Within a few seconds the rice swells—remove from heat immediately as soon as the rice starts to shift in colour from white to golden! Let rice drain on several layers of kitchen paper.

Crush the peanuts finely. Put aside. Peel and grate the ginger and squeeze out the ginger juice into a bowl. Discard the dry ginger. Combine the ginger juice with sugar, fish sauce, sesame oil and pressed lime. Skin the salmon and mince in food

2½fl oz (75ml) cooking oil
1¾oz (50g) uncooked basmati rice
3½oz (100g) peanuts
1 thumb-sized knob fresh ginger
½ tablespoon sugar
1 tablespoon fish sauce
1 teaspoon sesame oil (if you like)
3 limes
13oz (400g) salmon fillet
4 garlic cloves

processor. Chop the garlic finely. Fry the garlic in a bit of oil, add the salmon mince and fry quickly until it is done. Add the dressing, stir in the rice and peanuts and serve with noodles and steamed vegetables.

To compare cooking to lovemaking has always been popular, especially among male chefs of a certain red-faced, macho kind—and they're probably not all that mistaken. You can cook with or without love, with or without passion.

One could look at the act of cooking as a rather meaningless stretch towards the satisfied climax resulting from a consumed meal. And one could conclude that the initial activities involving the chef's skilled hands and mouth often makes the experience more intense for everyone involved.

However, I'm sad to say that this dish is *very hard* to cook with love. Not because the recipe doesn't deserve it. But because you've barely begun the act of cooking before its over and done with.

Lemon baked fish *with tomato and basil*

Preheat the oven to 500°F (250°C/Gas Mark 9) grill.

Slice tomatoes. Wash the lemons and grate the zest with a light and gentle hand (just the yellow part, no pith). Slice the garlic cloves very, very finely. Tear the leaves off the basil.

Combine olive oil, lemon zest, garlic, honey and salt in a bowl, add tomatoes and basil and stir gently. Line an ovenproof dish with baking paper and distribute the tomato

16oz (500g) cherry
  tomatoes
3 lemons
3 garlic cloves
2 pots of basil
3 tablespoons olive oil
1 tablespoon runny
  honey
1 teaspoon salt
4 individual fish fillets

mixture evenly. Salt and pepper the fish fillets, and place them on top. Slice the zested lemons thinly and use the slices to cover fish.

Cook fish in the oven for about 15 minutes or a little longer, depending on how thick the fish fillets are. Serve with couscous, bulgur, pasta or potatoes.

There's a fine line between being smart and being lazy. The most inventive and brilliant minds are rarely fuelled by their *desire to create*; instead it is their *reluctance to make an effort* that propels new, better, often simpler solutions to old, tricky problems. For instance, let's take a look at the art of making fine meatballs. *Back in the day*, you had to chop onions and hassle with spices. *These days:* remove the lid from a jar of pesto.

The business of cooking a tomato sauce and shaping the meat into little round balls certainly remains, there's no denying that. *But who knows?* In an upcoming cookbook, I might take this recipe to the next level so that all you have to do is to roll one single, huge ball that we'll all get to eat straight from the pot, standing by the stove. Or lying next to the pot on the kitchen floor. I'm keeping it open.

Pesto meatballs *in a tomato sauce*

Combine the pesto with the breadcrumbs and minced lamb. Season with salt and pepper and roll into balls.

Chop the garlic finely, fry in a little bit of olive oil, add the tomatoes and the water. Wash lemons and grate the zest with a light and gentle hand (just the yellow part, no pith). Add the zest from both lemons but only juice from one (or take a little more if you like) into the sauce. Taste and season with honey, salt and freshly ground pepper.

Drop the meatballs into the simmering tomato sauce. Gently shake the saucepan so

3½oz (100g) green pesto
1¾oz (50g) breadcrumbs
13oz (400g) lean lamb, minced
4 garlic cloves
2 cans passata or chopped tomatoes
2¾fl oz (100ml) water
2 lemons
2 tablespoons honey
2½oz (75g) pine nuts

that all the meatballs are covered in sauce. Let meatballs simmer for about 4 minutes. Serve the meatballs with roasted pine nuts, freshly cooked pasta, couscous or potatoes.

I've invented this recipe especially for those of you who spend your summers working as a chef in Greece. You'll find that this dish is new, fresh, exciting and yet strangely familiar. It's a dish that may seduce you into trying your hand at something that's not grilled into oblivion or fried in olive oil for so long that it's hard to remember what it once was.

This dish doesn't even call for the food to be arranged on skewers, nor should it be served with French fries or tzatziki. But, you say (with your eyes wide from astonishment), do you really mean there are Greek dishes beyond the twelve dishes in total that have been repeated over and over for as long as there have been charter tourists travelling to this part of the world?

And if that should be the case, *why waste energy on unnecessary inventions when there is gyros and souvlaki?*

Greek chicken stew *with feta cheese and olives*

Cut the chicken into 4–6 pieces, remove the skin (though you can let it remain on the wings) and trim away and discard any visible fat.

Fry the chicken in a little olive oil in a large pot. Remove the chicken and wipe the pot clean. Chop the garlic finely and fry in a little olive oil in the pot over medium heat. Add the chicken, pour over the canned tomatoes and wine and let simmer under the lid for at least 45 minutes.

Add balsamic vinegar and cherry tomatoes and let simmer for a few minutes. Taste the sauce and season with salt, freshly ground black pepper and perhaps a teaspoon of honey

1 organic chicken
4 garlic cloves
1 tin chopped
   tomatoes or passata
8¾fl oz (250ml) dry
   white wine
½ tablespoon balsamic
   vinegar
13oz (400g) cherry
   tomatoes
8oz (250g) authentic
   Greek feta cheese
3½oz (100g) black
   olives (with pits)

if you think the sauce is too sour. Dice the feta cheese or simply break it into pieces. Add feta and olives, gently heat and serve with couscous, bulgur or potato wedges.

Greek chicken stew *with feta cheese and olives* **163**

There are times when I think about *the meeting salad*, a cold mix of stale pasta, wet Parma ham, some lettuce leaves, one or two cherry tomatoes and a few hard balls of "mozzarella" unlovingly stuffed into a clear plastic bowl with a lid. Since the meeting salad is the very antithesis of anything even slightly imaginary, passionate, original or brave, it has become a top choice whenever a group of anxious adults meet up to kill a great idea only to replace it with a *strategic target market analysis* (code for something vague and harmless that no one could possibly care about).

The meeting salad is also available in the flavours *roast beef, curry chicken* and *shrimp with half an egg*. The going price for a meeting salad is £6–7, delivery charges and the cost of human suffering not taken into account.

Baked vegetables *with grapes, goat's cheese and sausage*

Preheat the oven to 440°F (225°C/Gas Mark 7). Trim and dice the vegetables—the softer, more watery the bigger chunks and vice versa. Place sausages, vegetables and grapes in a roasting pan or large ovenproof dish, sprinkle with pine nuts and flake salt and drizzle with a bit of olive oil. Cook in oven for about 30 minutes, turn the knob to grill and remove the dish from the oven once the veggies acquire beautiful, lightly burnt tips.

Cut goat's cheese in four slices, take the pan out of the oven and place the cheese on top of the vegetables, drizzle maple syrup over it all and put back on top rack of oven.

Serve as soon as the cheese takes on a beautifully golden colour.

4–6 uncooked chorizo, salsiccia or merguez
about 4lb (2kg) mixed vegetables of your choice, such as leeks, cauliflower, aubergine (eggplant), onion, fennel, pointed cabbage, peppers (capsicum), parsnip, carrots, endives, broccoli, butternut squash
10oz (300g) grapes
2½oz (75g) pine nuts
1 tablespoon maple syrup
flake salt
10oz (300g) goat's cheese

I'm not sure about this, but I strongly suspect that the mussel is, biologically speaking, related to the egg. Both species are characterised by their peculiar texture in their uncooked state, both are rich in protein and cholesterol, both live an anonymous, quiet life enclosed in shells. And since neither egg nor mussel seem to be doing anything exciting inside, you don't have to struggle with a guilty conscience for consuming them.

Sure, there are differences between the two, differences that contradict my theory. Mussels grow on ropes and on stones in the sea, while eggs grow under the bellies of hen. Another vital distinction between the two is that mussels, contrary to eggs, can't be used for baking.

And mussels are a much better choice when making soup.

Moules *with anise, potato wedges and baked fennel*

Preheat the oven to 400°F (200°C/Gas Mark 6). Scrub (or peel) and cut the potatoes into wedges. Trim the fennel from tough side shoots and the base of the root, then cut in 1-inch (2cm) thick slices. Place evenly in a pan, sprinkle generously with flake salt and top with thin slices of cold butter (use a potato peeler).

Put in oven for about 30 minutes, then turn the knob to grill. Remove from oven once the potatoes and fennel are beautifully golden with a few slightly burnt tips.

De-beard and scrub mussels. Discard any damaged mussels and those that won't close their shells when you gently tap them.

Chop the onion finely and the garlic even finer. Sweat onion and garlic in olive oil till translucent. Crush the fennel seeds in a mortar before you add them to the fried

32oz (1kg) potatoes
2 fennel bulbs
butter
4lb (2kg) mussels
2 onions
3 garlic cloves
1 teaspoon fennel
    seeds
4 whole star anise
2 tablespoons
    vegetable stock
    concentrate
2 lemons
1 orange
25fl oz (700ml) water
10fl oz (300ml) double
    cream

onions together with whole star anise. Let sizzle for a minute, add vegetable stock concentrate and let sizzle a little more.

Wash the lemons and the orange and grate the zest with a light and gentle hand (just the yellow part, no pith). Squeeze the citrus fruits and add the juice too—it may be enough with juice from the orange and just one lemon, so taste and decide for yourself. Add the water and bring to a boil. Does it look like the potatoes are almost done in the oven? Taste the soup and season with salt and freshly ground pepper.

Bring to a boil and add the mussels. Let them simmer for 5–7 minutes or until the shells are wide open. Rustle the pot a little every now and then to make sure the mussels cook evenly. Add the cream, stir and heat. Serve with potatoes and fennel.

Once upon a time, Christmas was illegal in England. And every now and then, you hear people saying that New Year's Eve should be outlawed, which is a reasonable thing to argue.

Of all holidays, people are really *in for it* this time of year. You spend a fortune on impractical garments. You drink too much. You text away until the stroke of midnight. You stand there, watching one firework after the other until your glass of champagne has frozen to the palm of your hand and has to be removed by trained professionals with the help of a weld. You spend hours on the phone waiting for someone to pick up your call for a taxi. You carry out the evening's longest (and least rewarding conversation) with a doorkeeper. You wake up the next morning to find that your wallet is missing.

And then you repeat this scenario year after year until suddenly, one day, you're old enough to examine your destructive New Year's habits. You decide it would be so much nicer to simply invite a few funny people and eat your way through the turn of the year—*if it wasn't for the New Year's dessert* and all the massive expectations of celebratory elegance that comes with it.

Where, oh *where* do you find a dessert that is more dignified than a pudding, more festive than ice cream and a little less expected than chocolate? Personally, I'll put my vote in favour of my own signature dessert. It should be accompanied by a fine port, and as long as you serve it with enough festive fruit you simply cannot fail with this dish, no matter how much champagne, wine and God knows what else you have diluted your blood with.

Then, when the moment arrives (be sure it will) and your guests ooh and aah, you just raise your glass of port, smile in an enigmatic way and discreetly change the topic of conversation.

Almond biscuits *with port and fruit*

Preheat the oven to 400°F (200°C/Gas Mark 6). Cut the almond paste in thin slices and sit them on baking trays lined with baking paper. Bake for about 8 minutes or until the cookies are nice and golden. Remove them

8oz (250g) almond paste
various fruits and berries
port

from the oven and set aside while you put in your best effort to arrange the fruit in an impressive manner on small plates.

Add cookies and serve with port on the side. Cheers!

Epilogue.

Once you have chewed your way through a 60-course meal, there's often some room left—for a hearty story. This one is true and is about the hungriest day of my life.

I had never been on a bicycle vacation before, nor had my sister. I can't recall if it was her or I that came up with such a silly idea and then successfully marketed domestic pedalling through forests, over fields and meadows as an adventurous and desirable undertaking.

In any case, we left the city a sunny July morning, on borrowed lady bicycles. In order to bring tents, sleeping bags, hair products, backpacking stove, posh dresses, worthwhile books, sunscreen and everything else you'd consider essential for a trip such as ours, we'd rented a bicycle trailer.

We managed to fit almost everything in the trailer, with the exception of the little repair kit in case of a flat tyre. Perhaps this was even a conscious strategy on our part, to invite adventure into our lives if fate would have it. Either way, we had been biking non-stop at a decent pace for six hours, when one of the wheels on our trailer suddenly burst. We stepped on our breaks, got off our bicycles; agreed the tyre was indeed very flat and that we were standing on a deserted country road.

Flat tyre. Two grumpy women. Loads of mosquitoes. And complete and utter silence.

"Why haven't we thought about food?" said Lina. She had a point, as you should always think about food.

Unfortunately, we had left the civilised world and all its splendid opportunities of endless eating far behind us. After a brief discussion, we decided to sit down by the roadside and wait for a farmer to putter by on a tractor and offer us food and fix the flat. The only trouble with our master plan was that no one showed up. No one at all.

"I think I hear someone coming."

We'd been waiting close to an hour when we heard the sound of a car approaching. Soon a vehicle came bouncing down the road, a worn down, muddy pick-up truck of the kind murderers drive in American movies. We ran down the road, waving our arms in the air. The car slowed down and came to a stop.

Suddenly, the window on the driver's side rolled down. We peeked inside. This is what we saw: an old man with a face that looked like a freshly ploughed field and a body so thin and frail that his overalls bagged everywhere.

"We have a flat tyre. On the trailer," Lina said, because somebody had to say something. Then, it happened very quickly. One moment our bikes were standing at the side of the road, the next they were loaded onto the pick-up and the rest of us were seated inside the car.

The next second we headed straight into the forest through a whirling chaos of spruce branches and anthills. The man at the wheel still hadn't said a word. We didn't talk either. It's hard to make light conversation as you're being thrown between the seat and roof of a car that's sputtering through the terrain so fast that moss is spraying against the trees.

After a while, possibly a few minutes, the forest parted to show a path that turned into a tractor track that turned into a gravel road that led to an open landscape and a white house surrounded by trash, old farming machines and stables.

Our car came to a screeching halt right in front of the house. Our chauffeur nodded towards the door on the passenger side and we stepped out. The air was filled with a smell of horses and rust. The car engine made strange ticking noises under the hood. When the front door opened, a large-sized woman dressed in riding boots, breeches and a very soiled bra stepped out onto the veranda. Behind us, the car started with a roar and left us in a cloud of dry gravel and exhaust fumes. *This doesn't feel great. Not at all*, I thought, and waved a little to show how nice and un-sad we were.

Let's be clear. The woman was a giant. She had a large, reddish face with a frowned forehead and squinty eyes. Broad shoulders where the bra straps made deep dents into her flesh, sturdy arms that hung flaccidly to her sides, ending in a pair of red, half-closed fists. One held a can of beer.

Without letting go of our sight, she raised the beer and took a few large gulps. At that instant, she shook as if a huge, heavy object had hit her at full force from behind; the pale roll of fat between bra and breeches seemed to jump as something big and hairy and terrible emerged between her leather clad thighs. Whatever it was, it had the same dimensions as a watermelon, loaded with gums and the sharp yellow teeth of a predator. It bellowed at us with such enthusiasm that saliva sprayed the steps.

I screamed. Lina screamed, everyone screamed—and the one who screamed the loudest was the woman, who insisted that the dog simply wanted to greet the guests.

"This is Arne," she added when the noise had calmed down. Then she patted the beast, which was supposedly a dog named Arne, between the eyes with her fist. Arne the dog unleashed his tongue and simultaneously let out a puddle of rubbery saliva.

"Welcome to Klastorp," the woman said and smiled for the first time since meeting us. "I'll go make some coffee."

Before we had a chance to reply she turned around and went back into the house. We remained in our spots and watched as Arne clawed the planks of the veranda in the hope of breaking the chain that kept him from taking a closer look at us. The sheer force in his efforts made the skin on the side of his head stretch until the pink insides of his eyelids were clearly visible.

We drank our coffee from cups that had likely never been washed, seated at the small patio in the shade behind the house, with a view of nettles, an old broken toilet and the remains of a kitchen interior.

We weren't served anything to eat. But Arne was. He chewed on the shinbone of an elk. Most likely, he had already eaten the rest of the animal. I could imagine how he'd started by chewing the rubbery muzzle, then methodically worked his way through the king of the forest, bit by bit. Now, all that remained was this little shank, a bone shaft with a joint at one end and a fur-clad hoof at the other.

"We were away for a day last fall, when a family came a little too close to our property. And you know Arne is a trained guard dog so he watched them for six hours, mum, dad and their two kids. They were done for when we returned!" said the woman, who by now had introduced herself as Bitten, letting out a roaring laugh.

It hadn't taken long for us to realise that any effort to converse Bitten in a regular fashion would be a waste of time.

She kept talking in a normal voice only to change into a strange, shrill baby voice. After a while, it was clear that the shrill voice belonged to Arne. Though the words came out of Bitten's mouth, it was really Arne having his say. This way, we were treated to Arne's hardships at the veterinary hospital, where he'd recently had been relieved of a bunch of fist-sized cancer rumours in his nether regions.

At some point Bitten, or perhaps Arne, asked about our professions. I replied that I was a copywriter working at an advertising agency, but that I dreamed about working with food. Bitten frowned and studied me closely before asking if it was easy getting a job at an advertising agency. Before I got a chance to reply, she changed the topic.

Once we'd finished our coffee, Lina and I obeyed Bitten's explicit demand to perform a "house warrant" (I know). First, we were sent around on our own. We had to visit the upstairs first "because that's where it's beautifulest". Sure. A bit dark perhaps. Red velvet wallpaper absorbed what little light had managed to find its way through the drawn curtains in brown, broad-gauge corduroy. The air had an old, weak taste, as if the entire floor had been hermetically sealed, the same air inhaled and exhaled by the inhabitants over a thousand sticky days and nights. I have never, not before nor later, visited a more dusty, dingy and red tinged place. In the corner, a heavy leather couch perspirated in the heat.

Next to the couch was a bar with a built-in mirror reflecting the labels on the bottles. Bar stools. A dartboard. No rugs with the exception of a bear hide on the floor, unmistakably authentic and, from its condition, home to every known species of bugs, mites and vermin. There were variations on the theme of animal heads on the wall— some carried full facial features while others showed only the horns of deceased elk and deer. The remaining surfaces were covered with cups, trophies, medals, bowls, plaques and rosette ribbons that Bitten had obviously won through equestrian triumphs. Lina estimated the total amount at 477 pieces. To top her, I put my guess at 616.

We almost made it to ten full minutes, but then we had to go downstairs to breathe. Bitten must have been standing there, listening for our footsteps from the bottom floor, calculated the minutes and then interpreted the scarce amount of time we had spent upstairs as an incredibly rude gesture of disinterest.

As she met us at the foot of the stairs, she kept her arms folded across her chest and her lips pressed together so hard that they'd lost all colour. We had no choice but to trot up the stairs once more to look more carefully. To make sure we looked properly, Bitten came with us. The guests should not miss anything noteworthy.

"This is where dad and I sleep," Bitten told us in a happy voice and pushed us into another room, even gloomier than the parlour room. Once our eyes had adjusted to the darkness, we could see a narrow double bed with four posters. The threadbare bedspread, tucked in tightly under the mattress, was of a faded brown colour, suspiciously similar to authentic dirt.

"And Arne, of course! Arne sleeps in the middle with us."

Next to the bed, someone had placed a small baby bed.

"And who sleeps there?" Lina asked.

"That's where our boy will sleep," Bitten said and explained contentedly, "We've adopted a 12-year-old from Russia. He'll be here two weeks from now."

She pronounced Russia as "Rrraschia" with a long, rolling R. My mouth had dried up completely. The previous few hours' sensations of hunger had now been replaced by fear—bona fide fear as in hard heartbeats, a distinct pressure over the chest and a tingling in my hands.

No one had seen us arrive at this place. No one even knew we were here. No one would miss us for over a week. I began to wish, intensely, that we'd never ventured out on a bicycle trip at all. I wished I had cancelled my vacation. I wished the bicycle had never been invented. But none of my wishes would come true this day. Instead, sightseeing erupted upon us.

First stop: The family hen farm. We were told it would take some time to get there, but Bitten had a car.

"One hundred meters of hen!" Bitten had to shout now, to make her voice heard through the cackle. "They're all doing just fine here!" she added.

The hen farm turned out to be a low tin box with no windows. It was, just as you might have guessed, jam packed with dusty white hens who had long ago crossed the border to a nervous breakdown and who were now busy taking each other out of their misery with the help of beaks and claws.

The next attraction was the stables, the building that had been the stable before the other stable became the stable and lastly the recently begun building of the new stable—so far just a wheelbarrow and a few poles under a tarp. We nodded and made little sounds that we hoped seemed complimentary while Bitten made elaborate explanations about all the great things she had planned for the future.

Next, we ventured out into a pen to search for a horse. There should be four of them, Duchesse, Crimson, Melissa and Chenille, and to leave the pen without saying hello to them was inconceivable. The pen was very large and every time we finally saw a horse, it saw us, rolled its eyes, thrust its head backwards and galloped away.

When each terrified horse had finally been seen and patted to Bitten's satisfaction, it was time for us to visit the special bus in which you transport your own fine self when you're participating in equestrian events all over Europe. I can assure you we inspected this bus with the meticulousness of ten crime investigators at a murder scene. No detail was too small or insignificant.

First, we were treated to a demonstration of the driver's seat. Then the passenger seats. And the beds, complete with pillows and mattresses. We looked at the trunk. We peeked into the small refrigerator. We looked at a blanket that was great to have, you know, when you're taking a little nap during very long drives.

Then we jumped in the car again and drove off to the paddock that Bitten and dad were building. They hadn't proceeded that far with the project but we assured her that we thought we got the idea. Then we went back to the white house again to look at three cats, a heap of bunny hutches and observe the contents of burlap bags with animal feed. We paid visits to Arne's dog shed and to the wonderful place where sparrows and tits could feast on tallow ball and sunflower seeds during the cold hard winter months.

We surveyed a field where Bitten and dad grew wheat, another where they grew rye, a painting by Bitten's grandfather and a photo album with pictures from Rrraschia. We saw a humorous magnet on the fridge and a postcard from a remote relative who was deceased these days and buried in a place, the location of which we were carefully informed of with the help of a map.

We were just about to receive a thorough display of a few broken horse bridles when dad emerged with the fixed tyre in his hand. Loads of money changed ownership and the wheel was put back on the trailer.

"Well, thank you so much for having us," I said once we sat on our bikes again.

Bitten grabbed onto my carrier. The afternoon's enthusiasm had began to give way, and when she started to describe the way we were supposed to bike, she looked very angry. Sure, the suggested route was a good two miles longer than the one we wanted to take, but if we didn't take the detour we'd miss our chance to see the house she and dad had lived in before they bought this house. We nodded—and as soon as she'd let go of my bike, we pedalled the other way, towards the main road, towards freedom, towards a life we so recently had thought would be lost to us forever.

Only once did I turn around. Bitten stood where we'd left her, her mouth opening and shutting and her arms making such large gestures the contents of her soiled bra rose and rolled. Arne pulled at his chain.

We pedalled our way forward, through the twilight landscape as the handlebars carved their ways into our palms, our thigh muscles tightened and our heads filled with air. We left the gravel roads behind us and found our way back to the asphalt. Bit by bit, the spruce stood wideapart, the roads became wider and the traffic more dense. Forest and fields gave way to industries and buildings.

Suddenly we could sense the city in the distance, and a thousand pains later, we arrived. It was like coming home, falling into a warm, welcoming embrace, oozing with exhaust fumes, frying oil and alcohol.

As we rolled into Stockholm, it was two in the morning and all the restaurants and bars had just spit out their last intoxicated guests. Outside the entrance to the subway, we saw the sad remains of a bachelor party; five men who had celebrated their friend by dressing him in lacy lingerie and flippers. On the other side of the street, a few gentlemen settled an argument with their fists. Their movements were slow and the majority of the punches hit only air, but after numerous efforts one of them finally produced some nose bleeding, an event accepted by all as the conclusion.

We made our way to the nearest street stand and joined the temperamental crowd that all wanted just one final bite before missing the last bus home. The line was very long. The couple in front of us argued about something. The couple behind us argued too. At this point, we were not above a little arguing ourselves. We just couldn't muster the energy to do so.

Finally, it was our turn. The lady behind the counter was in her sixties. The hardened type. Red hair, thin lips and a large mustard stain on her apron. Lina ordered a quarter pounder with cheese, garlic dressing and coleslaw. Personally, I went for four grilled sausages with ketchup, mustard and roasted onions.

But before we proceed, let me pause to tell you one more thing before this book reaches the end. *I love food.* I love eating it, cooking it and I love being the person putting the dinner on the table so that we can sit down, eat and talk a little. Because food and talk and great and not-so-great stories go hand in hand. We meet up around food, eat it and entertain each other until our plates are scraped clean. It's not really about anything more. But that's more than enough.

The sausages were so freshly grilled I could hear them making snapping crackling sounds from deep under all the layers of ketchup and condiments glittering in the faint yellow light of the street lamps. We found a bench to sit on, miraculously free from food spills. Then we ate. We ate and ate and ate. When we'd finished every last piece of food, we sat on the bench a little bit longer and promised each other never to bike again. And now we've arrived at the very end of the story of the most delicious meal I've eaten in my entire life.

Thanks for the food.

INDEX OF ALL THE RECIPES

INDEX OF ALL THE INGREDIENTS

£25.00

THANK YOU.
Thanks to all the *readers* who found me on the web,
read my words and kept telling me to make this book.
Thanks to *Garbergs* for lending me your most precious co-workers,
Thanks to *Lotta Agaton*, *NK* Kök, Glas & Porslin, *Vikingsun*,
Tofte and *Barbro* for lending us props,
Thanks *Independent Kostym* and *Twilfit* for clothes,
Thanks *Lina Lundgren* for the Asian chicken salad,
Thanks *Thelma/Louise* for the little movie,
Thanks *Timo Räisänen* and *Hans Olsson Brooks* for the soundtrack for the movie,
Thanks *Martin* for always eating and
Thanks *Josephine Cochrane* for inventing the dishwasher,

£25.00